THE WRITING WORLD
Living the Literary Life

DELMA LUBEN

D0623442

HALLYN PRESS
Phoenix, Arizona

THE WRITING WORLD

Most of the chapters in this book have appeared in "Writing and Selling," the author's monthly column as contributing editor for Writer's World Magazine.

"How To Survive In The Writing World" was originally published as a cover feature in Byline Magazine (May 91)

All poems in this book have been previously published (some in slightly different form)--in **Poems For Poets And Writers** © 1990, Delma Luben, and in various issues of the following magazines: *Authorship, Chips off the Writer's Block, Clockwise, Cross and Quill, Crystal Rainbow, Explorer, Mind In Motion, Mobius, Muse Portfolio, New Author's Journal, Perceptions, The Poet's Edge, Purpose, Silver Wings, Thumbprints, Writer's Haven, Writer's Gazette, Writer's Newsletter, and Writer's World.*

Library of Congress Catalog Card Number: 2001094381
ISBN 0-9712411-0-4

Printed in the United States of America

To all the good writers out there
who are not <u>yet</u> published.

ACKNOWLEDGMENTS

With heartfelt gratitude, I hereby publicly pay tribute to the late Susy Smith for twenty-three years of friendship and support. By her cooperative sharing of knowledge, expertise, and extensive experience, my writing career progressed. By her example, I try to pass it on to others.

And kudos to all my students. Through the years your interest, response, and related experiences often provided input for my courses and presentations. Thanks, also, for the letters and phone calls keeping me apprised of your progress.

LIVING THE LITERARY LIFE

Dreaming of money
and adulation,
writers submerged
in isolation
(living on
crumbs of hope)
exist in reflection
of their creation
by periscope.

CONTENTS - PROSE

Introduction . . .

CONTENTS - POETRY

Living the Literary Life . . .

INTRODUCTION

"Those who wish to succeed must ask
the right preliminary questions."

-- Aristotle

This book was compiled to help answer some of the right preliminary questions that many beginning writers fail to ask--until an avalanche of rejection rains on their enthusiasm and drowns their confidence. Also for the "more than a million" Americans who suffer from writer's itch, but for fear of rejection dare not try. And especially for those long-trying residents of the writing world who spend more time suffering than smiling. Through the years I've met so many of you . . .

Not sidetracked by convention pulls or play, you read, study, work night and day, but still don't see your dreams coming true. So now you're reading yet another book, in search of the elusive answers.

I sincerely hope you find some of them here. My purpose in writing this book is to help prevent some of the angst and agony writers inevitably encounter. **The Writing World** is less about how to write, more about what to expect, and how to survive until you succeed. In this eclectic selection of need-to-know information, second-hand philosophies, and different recipes for progress may you also find ideas for maintaining your balance (on the seesaw of hope and rejection), and for keeping up your confidence.

While climbing the ladder to professional writer, that dreamer self-assurance is easily lost. Every day writers on every step, as well as students on the first rung, lose faith in their talent and fall off. And all too often it's for believing a fable. "Learn to write well and publication will follow."

This is a dream-killer assumption.

Without seeing your work I can assure you there is worse writing out there. Poor writing is frequently published. Most is mediocre. To quote Logan Pearsall Smith, "A best-seller is the gilded tomb of a mediocre talent." Believe him. It is not artistic ability that makes money, but ability to sell-- knowing the publishing business, and how to build sensation (to capture the masses), plus promotion, promotion, promotion…

The editor may censure your effort, but most readers won't know, or care, if it's good writing. They never did. Back in another century Emerson said, "People do not deserve good writing, they are so pleased with bad."

Still, for a writer the bottom line is good writing (making it as good as we can). But for the publisher, the bottom-line is the bottom line. Those authors (good and bad) who beat you to print did it by learning the tricks of the publishing trade. The major prerequisites for published author also include ferreting out right editors, and allotting up to thirty percent of your time to the mundane job of marketing. When plotting the path to your goal keep in mind that the vast majority of modern publishers are not lovers of literature; they're entrepreneurs; the plurality of books is not art to be treasured but products to be marketed. As you realize this, and are able to ascertain what happens to your manuscript on the other side of the editor's desk--when you get the whole picture--then you'll start seeing acceptances.

But a caveat, prepare for a long haul.

Becoming a writer isn't smooth sailing. Every famous author did time in the school of trial and error. No matter how diligently you study and practice, don't think you can skip it. Rejection is inevitable for everybody. Nobody sells everything--even after a best seller. That's how it is. And perhaps how it was meant to be, for rejection is our greatest teacher.

This was indelibly impressed on my mind early. At a writing seminar I hung on the words of a first book author (after seven years of trial and error) who seemed to be answering my every unspoken question. But nothing *said* stayed with me like the ending demonstration. Concluding his speech, Harry E. Neal (who later published eighteen more books) opened a briefcase and withdrew a large wad of what looked like rolled up fabric and ragged paper.

"Now," he said, "I'm going to show you, not just tell you, what it takes to become a writer."

Handing one end to a surprised man on the front row, he slowly walked to the far end of the stage carefully unfolding, revealing an uncountable number of papers in various sizes and colors stapled like laundry on a red ribbon clothesline.

His rejection slips!

Nothing could have been more effective. Witnessing those paper stepping-stones to success, how could the aspiring authors in his audience forfeit their dreams for having received only a dozen or so?

How can you?

With determination you will reach your goal if you write well, learn the publishing business, and be patient. Remember, a novice evolves into a professional; you don't get promoted on a time scale. And a word about the negativity here, and other places in the book … Where the black and white of it is mostly black, that's what you get-- to arm you against any unrealistic assumptions. Within these pages you will find no facts or related situations colored rosy. I saved that color for your future.

And what a great future it can be. Every plus and minus considered, there is no more interesting, exciting career than "freelance writer." I'm betting you agree, or you wouldn't be reading this. Also I'm assuming that you've read many other books on writing; and after gleaning all you can from this one, I hope you will continue reading them. For every one will be part review and part discovery. As you select from the mix, each with a different presentation, depending on your state of mind, what you're working on at present, how the details are presented, odds are that something you've been confused about will all at once become clear! This "suddenly the light goes on" even happens to seasoned writers. There's no point where we stop learning, especially about the ever-changing game of publishing.

The difference between success and failure as a writer is not just artistic ability. Reading, study, and practice master the art of writing; but earning the title of "author" also mandates a thorough knowledge of the other side of the business. As artists, most writers are inherently averse to commercialism (and the mundane job of selling) but to be read we must remember what Robert Louis Stevenson said.

"Everybody lives by selling something."

You are proud of your creations; you want to share them with the world; then come down from your ivory tower and go to bat for them. Just as the thrill of creating cannot be compared to any other vocation, promoting and selling are never beneath those who are proud of what they create.

In this collection I've tried to paint true pictures of living and working as a writer. If you are experienced, but frustrated, I hope you find them helpful. If you're just beginning may they give you a jump-start. If you've not yet dared to begin, start now. We all learn as we go.

BRIGHT OCCASSION

I am here
and it is now—
what an opportunity!

THE FIRST COMMANDMENT OF SUCCESS

What is the one common denominator among people who achieve their highest goals? They all, without exception, keep the first commandment of success--work.

The first man was sent forth out of a workless garden and admonished "By the sweat of your face you shall eat bread." God decreed it; the all-time best seller mentions it over 350 times. All best sellers result from it. Hard continuous work has no stand-in, no substitute; it tops the list of fame and fortune requisites. Networking and getting along with people ranks near the top, even with loners called writers; we must get along with editors. Yet there are celebrity authors who don't know how. Education and special training are invaluable; but uneducated novelists have made millions. Sometimes the winners seem to posses no special talent or genius . . .

The name of the game these people play?

Work.

George Bernard Shaw said, "When I was a young man I observed that nine out of ten things I did were failures. I didn't want to be a failure, so I did *ten times more work.*"

"By dint of hard work," Adela Rogers St. Johns earned the title, "most successful woman author of her time." She died working, at 94.

At 78 Upton Sinclair had published 90 books. He gave this advice to young writers. "Work. Study hard, think for yourself, and work."

As the successful repeatedly tell us, the constantly working turtle passes everybody, even the genius. And luck is preordained by work. Writers who meet the typewriter or computer at dawn, or midnight, and exert indefinitely, like laborers who start at five a.m. and toil 'till dark, have the best chance of getting lucky. When a millionaire (who once was a laborer) wrote his "Ten Commandments of Success," *hard work* topped the list.

But what if it tops your list and you're not free to write--can't start writing until the end of a wage-earning day, are forced by family duty to quit early, have no privacy, or peace and quiet?

Nobody ever said becoming a writer is easy. For most of us it's rebellion against someone insisting we should be something else, against our practical side dictating, or we're fighting the colorful, powerful forces of commercialism that so often imprison artistic desire.

All during my career in administrative management and public relations for The Government, I tried to down "the divine discontent" for the good money. It was not possible. Every spare minute I thought studied dreamed writing. When finally free to follow the pull I recognized the long lonely road ahead of me--but had no idea of the myriad boulders that would block my way.

If you have chosen this road and something or somebody inhibits you, while you're thwarted be studying. Practice when you can. Write earlier; write longer. Steal time from sleep and play. If you really want to be an author you can't take your writing too seriously.

Tom Robbins said, "we must maintain a pitch next to madness..."

And as we work fervently to build our creative ability into a positive power we must remember to protect the source of that power. Our physical health. However great the aspiration, physical breakdown forfeits the dream. Those who win in spite of ill health are rare; those who lose because of it are countless.

Keep your body and mind healthy with good food, good care, good habits. Exercise. Immune yourself against worry and tension. Stay able to pay the hard work price. This expensive price tag on success weeds out the weak and the pretenders; the real writers stay and pay, and keep paying.

Dickens was lucky. He burned the candle at both ends and lived to enjoy the glow. His breakdown came *after* fame. Still he worked, when he "felt as if ... already dead."

Tolstoy, reportedly "...hanging on by his nerves" after working night and day for six long years on *War and Peace*, made so many changes and improvements on the manuscript proofs the typesetter bills became exorbitant. The editor despaired. "If you go on like this we will be correcting forever. Half your changes are unnecessary, for love of God, stop!" Yet Tolstoy worked on--to make a masterpiece better.

Famous authors don't all possess more talent, or anything else that we don't. The best of them doubt and suffer as we do. The difference? They work harder, and longer. If you do likewise, and confidently proceed in the direction of your dream, the brighter day *will* dawn. By die-hard dedication, and the magic tonic called work, you too could one-day see your masterpiece read by the world.

The wonders of work make history, enough effects miracles! The first commandment of success, decree for planet earth: "By the sweat of your face you shall eat bread."

How much bread do you want?

WRITER IN TRAINING

Living with the muse,
listening with the heart,
developing patience
and a thicker skin,
learning to balance
rejection/acceptance,
working, writing,
dreaming the chance,
slowly, slowly
perfecting the dance
--becoming a writer.

WHAT DOES IT TAKE?

What does it take to become a professional writer?

To become a "complete novelist," Leon Uris says "it takes the concentration of a Trappist monk, the organizational ability of a Prussian field marshal, the insight into human relations of a Viennese psychiatrist, the discipline of a man who prints the Lord's Prayer on the head of a pin..."

Novelist Kate Braverman told an interviewer it takes "the stamina of a channel swimmer and the faith of a fanatic."

James Thurber, speaking to an audience of aspiring writers, said that it takes "talent, application, and aspirin."

And everyone tells you it takes *time*.

But there is another very important requisite, seldom mentioned--the ability to successfully balance your writing life and your family life.

Victims of this craving to create, unless they live alone and have no friends, must realize that a writing career requires rearrangement of their lives. It mandates a change in mental, physical, and personal habits. It also presents what may be the writer's greatest challenge--learning to deal with the myriad distractions, interruptions, and misunderstandings.

No matter how many times I tell non-writing friends that I "work" until noon, they still call mornings--and when they get the answering machine, want to know where I was. Although my family agreed not to interrupt me (except for an emergency) still they do. And after every interruption, inevitably, the response to my fated frown of impatience goes something like this. "But it will just take a minute!"

Does this sound familiar to you? Do people in your household often interrupt your chain of thought? Does someone repeatedly ask you to take a day, or an hour off? Or suggest a vacation without considering (or even remembering) your deadline date? If so, do you acquiesce for peace in the family? If you don't, do you feel guilty?

It takes patience and practice to learn to communicate on paper, and equally as much to communicate the damage of distraction to a non-writer. When we lose an idea that just surfaced, or the perfect phrase we were mentally refining, it's hard not to respond irritably. Few of us can manage a smile and act as if it didn't matter. So we must try to reduce or eliminate these situations. If you are having trouble obtaining family cooperation you might try Jimmy Carter's solution.

After the president retired to Georgia his wife Rosalynn kept friends and family at bay while he wrote a book. But no one returned the favor when she wrote one--until one day after the third interruption in an hour she ran from the room crying. When she returned Jimmy had put a sign on her door. "DO NOT DISTURB, working hours 9-12." And thereafter he ran interference for her, insisting on family cooperation. From then on even her mother respected her writing hours.

Don't neglect your family, or your duties. Set a time to write when your you are least needed (if it's midnight to six a.m.). Work it out with their schedules. Then when your agreed-to understanding is not honored, firmly remind the people you live with of their part in the dual commitment. If you don't, if you allow yourself be intimidated you'll wind up with nothing but a ready-made list of excuses for your lack of progress. Like these I hear from my students when they haven't completed an assignment.

"My husband keeps coming in; sometimes he breaks my concentration just to ask which shirt I think he should wear!"

"This morning my wife came upstairs bearing a treat; she thought I needed a break. I never got back to it."

"I've told my daughter I don't want to take any calls, but…"

How do you handle these situations?

Explaining your priorities without seeming to put your loved ones second is a real communication challenge, requiring a just right selection of words. It's a hard job for a communications professional, and you are still learning. So how are you doing? If someone calls you to the telephone after you've explained why you turn down the ringer, and don't have an extension in your office, it's hard to calmly explain again. Can you hide your exasperation when expected to make an exception? When they say, "but it's…" (your mother or a close friend) do you sigh and take the call? If not, can you be firm and say something that hides your irritation?

You are in for the long haul, and if you aren't blessed to have a special, secluded, off-limits place to write, it's imperative to convince the people in your household that you are unavailable during writing time. Somehow you must make them understand that it's the same as if you "went to work."

John Updike rented an office downtown. Many top authors have their private office or cabin. Others handle the family and friends problem by disappearing entirely. However, not telling anyone where your hideaway is can be risky. A writer I know went this route, and began selling regularly; but she was divorced for it.

When you opt for a writing career you know you will have to discipline yourself; you learn that you also need to discipline your family. Those who work under the umbrella of supportive loved ones are lucky; they're fortified to withstand even torrents of rejection. But those plagued by stormy emotional weather may be psychologically unable to stay afloat, even in a moderate sea of negativity. If you're flailing in these waters you *must* find a way to alter the situation. Or quit.

In an open letter to victims of family indifference, *Writer's Forum* editor Alexander Blackburn said, "If you can quit you probably should."

If you can't, don't give up your dream. Consider the situation a challenge that other writers have conquered; you can too. Only the lucky (with a hideaway), or the hermit fail to hear the every day arguments. "But we'd only be gone an hour... "But it's the first day of spring ... "But this is the once a year big sale!"

We can't understand how non-writers consider these things more worthy of our time. They can't believe that we'd rather write. Different thinking, different values—and like a mile between!

It has been said that family and friends are the writer's enemy. This cannot be. Work out a compromise. Have a family conference. Tell everybody how much writing means to you. Be honest, open, and convincing. Share your dream. Unless you do, unless you learn to live in harmony, you may not make it.

For your success, and peace of mind, that's what it takes.

HOW IT IS

What you pay
for a writing career,
with rare bestseller
exception, is far
out of proportion
to what you receive.

Remuneration
is often nil.
While the mind soars
the body sits
(sometimes to petrifying).
You suffer bouts of
poverty, worry,
alienated family . . .

That's how it is.
But if you're meant
to be a writer,
whatever--
and however long,
you'll hang in there
until you sing your song.

WHEN WE ACCEPT THE LOAD

Responsibility.

It's a big word, and a heavy load to carry. When we're given it we grow stronger and better at what we do. When we fully accept it we succeed.

With the realization that you have but one boss, yourself, you're on the right road, and well on your way. This truism is particularly pertinent to writers—as applicable as it is for top leaders.

According to presidential advisor Bernard Baruche, acceptance of responsibility is the one quality that raises talent to the top--and keeps it there. He advised the nation's highest leaders, "Don't blame anyone for your mistakes and failures."

Blaming is an inherent human tendency. When we flub up or fall short we usually look for someone or something to share the responsibility. This impulse plagues executives. Surrounded by "yes men" and willing patsies they can as easily delegate blame as duties. But freelance writers (no staff or ready supporters) must carry the full load to the pinnacle. For this we need strong shoulders. And it's never too early to start developing them.

The first day of a new writing class I ask attendees to fill out a form which includes the questions "How long have you been writing?" And "What, if anything, have you published?" From the consensus of their answers I determine how basic the course needs to be. Inevitably, there will be added reasons (excuses) for not having written, or published. Usually one of the following.

Spouse does not cooperate
Have to work long hours
Didn't get to go to college
Don't have a computer

Do you use some of these common circumstance excuses for not having done what you want most to do? Not only novices play the excuse game. Almost every unmotivated would-be writer makes excuses a habit.

Or they inhibit themselves with a mind-set on the impossibility of publishing. I know an author who has fallen back to the practice, after twenty-two published books. Once her family-values stories sold easily. Now, after seven years without a sale, deep in the pit of rejection, she wails, "All they want nowadays is sex and murder," and gives up. Rather than submit to the necessary hours of market study to ferret out the rare receptive editors/publishers, who *might* print her work, she blames society, and ends her career.

Don't let your career end this way. It isn't a perfect world; injustice and inequity often reign. Why should we expect the writing world to be different? If you encounter unfairness, suffer bad luck, get a "dirty deal," complaining won't level the scale. Your Jerico walls won't fall down for crying (or praying); you must find a way around them, with or without help. For no one else, no mentor, no kind professor, not even your mother cares as much. You are the one who wants to be a writer.

When luck breaks against you resolve not to dwell on it. Maintain a one-track mind zeroed in on what you're writing, and hang in there no matter what. That's what professionals do. My friend the late western writer Mike Wales is a prime example. Author of the popular "Leatherhand Series," he signed a contract for four more books *after* his doctor told him he had six months to live.

"I try not to think about how much time I've got," he said, "I just keep working; I want to get as many as I can to my editor." He finished three.

Of course a new writer submitting to an unknown editor will not be spurred by such promptings of loyalty. For the beginner it's more like sending a test paper. If you pass you qualify for the job you've worked and studied for. If you do everything right, you'll receive an acceptance--that's what you've been told. But you learn that sometimes fate flunks you.

You do your homework, find a just-right publication, study sample copies, follow guidelines to the letter . . . And the writing goes well; deep inside you know it's good. This time, you feel sure of an acceptance.

Then doom—the situation was out of your control.

The newly appointed editor does not adhere to details his predecessor furnished for the market listing. A previous issue (before the one or two samples you studied) contained an article on the same subject. The magazine folded after the listing was published . . . There could be myriad reasons.

But whatever, whose fault was it that you didn't know these things? Think about it. The reason may have been knowable with a little more effort. You could have read *three* issues; you could have called to confirm the name of the editor, you could have … you could have … Keep in mind that the situation constantly changes. Make last minute checks. And consider the possibility of error on the receiving end: editor turnover, the short life of many publications … There are hundreds of potential reasons for a no sale, many of which remain unknown to the writer. Learn to accept and forget.

While a known mistake of yesterday becomes your lesson for today, from an unknown one you go on wiser, and keep learning, and keep going.

Mona Van Duyn, America's first female poet laureate (June 1992-93) told an interviewer that she made it to the top because "I just kept going." No breaks, no help, no special equipment, she simply "put everything else out of my head and kept working." Van Duyn wrote her prize-winning poetry in long hand, while cooking for a family on an outdated gas stove and sewing her own clothes on a 1950 sewing machine. At the time she was honored with the appointment, she still didn't own a computer or word processor.

By ignoring the negative (what she was missing) and accepting the full load, playwright/poet Maya Angelou climbed up out of poverty and segregation to "Inaugural Poet" for President Clinton.

Such accomplished poets and writers possess power to influence lives.

Many, like Harriet Beecher Stowe, Sinclair Lewis, Rachel Carson made a definite contribution to humanity. To aid in human progress is the serious writer's mission. If you harbor this high aspiration forget inequity and inefficiency. Block them out. Label your backsets, "experience" (every one) and build on them. Waste no time trying to identify the culprit, take the load on your shoulders accept it, carry it, and keep going. Assessing blame slows learning, drains energy, and gains you nothing. Shifting responsibility is the devil's advocate that lures writers down the black alley of depression leading to quitting.

Too many times I've seen it happen.

Long association with all kinds of writers at every level, and hard experience, have convinced me that no exception can justify the shifting of responsibility. If you would be a winner, a professional well paid writer, remember those ten most powerful two-letter words.

"If it is to be, it is up to me."

Accept the load.

THE UNCOLORED CANVAS

When you stand in
the serene stillness
of dawn, ready
to paint your day,
do you remember
that *you* are the artist?

Do you paint your life
your way?

Or let other
painters dole out
colors you will play,
twist the purity,
bend your thoughts,
delete your
individuality?

When you face the
uncolored canvas, ready
to paint for humanity,
do you resist the wind
of convention?

Can you stand true to
the voice within?

RELAX—WRITE IT YOUR WAY

Have you ever taken a public speaking course? What did the instructor tell you first? And emphasize most? If more writing instructors emphasized this I firmly believe beginning writers would publish sooner.

Relax. Be yourself. Just talk to your audience.

The serious beginner lives in constant fear that an editor will spot him as an amateur. He studies, worries, dreams of a wonder drug that will make him remember every detail. And with every rejection tries harder—until he becomes so up tight he writes like a robot.

If you've been straining for years, rigidly following rules, and haven't sold anything, you may be trying too hard. It is entirely possible to be too cold-fact correct. You must present your work according to written rules; you must slant, and write what *they* want; but write it your way.

Don't clone your teacher or favorite author. Just try to write to the heart of your reader.

The significant difference between a successful writer and a struggler is the ability to touch the mind and heart—to be human on paper. And remember your first reader, an acquisitions editor, is human too. She is not a scoring machine. According to the guest editor at a recent writing seminar, if your article or story is not well organized, if it doesn't flow, if the topic is too general but in some way it touches her, she will want to work with you to make the piece acceptable. "But," she said, "if it projects no feeling, or personal uniqueness, it isn't worth the trouble."

Do you keep those form letter rejection slips, and keep trying to read between the lines, hoping to learn something, that so often isn't there? If so, go pull out a few of the quick check variety, and this time note the many reasons (ready for the editor's selection) that have nothing to do with the mechanics of writing.

> Didn't make us laugh/cry
> Needs a more personal focus
> Failed to move us
> Brings no freshness to the subject
> Lacking in feeling

In talking with new writers I find the majority over-oriented on fact, under-oriented on feeling. They study procedure, worry about correct grammar, structure, manuscript mechanics—knowing that *right* reigns as the utter acceptance factor …

But what is right?

Beyond the basics it's peculiar to the editor; whereas all editors clamor for personality writing. Without any personal punches your slanted, carefully selected words will slouch there on the paper like a long gray line of tedium. And the editor won't read to the end of them.

What whetted your appetite to write on that subject? What stirred your insides? Let it come through. It's this distinctive inner voice that arrests an editor's attention.

The first time I dared to allow my inner voice, on an article I called "You Are What You Think," the writing went so well I thrilled, sixth sense certain that the piece would sell. But before I mailed it someone gave me a copy of James Allen's *As A Man Thinketh*. Clouds of doubt came down on my assurance. I hadn't read the classic, but here were all my ideas. Where did I get them? From my subconscious? From other writings? I didn't know. I just knew that I could not submit that article. Then an old pro reminded me that everything's been done. "We just have to do it differently."

She convinced me that not only could I send it, but that it would sell. And it did, first time out!

Nelson Algren, called one of the finest living writers (circa 1900) said, "Success comes when you learn to perceive life with originality and are daring enough to put it down as you see it."

If you've tried everything else dare to be you. Loosen up; let your ideas flow. Stamp your work private property. Leave your fingerprints all over it. Then begin thinking of the editor as someone you would like to meet instead of a potential enemy. Editors want to meet you, through the work you submit to them. Of course try to make a good impression; but don't be intimidated; imagine the editor you're submitting to as a friend. And relax.

A man named Tom Bodett, when a college writing teacher told him to "write just the way you talk," relaxed, quit studying, and went home to produce a successful radio show. Someone from an ad agency, recognizing his personal sparkle, commissioned him to tape a Motel-6 commercial. Still just talking, he ad-libbed, "We'll leave the light on for ya…"

The rest of his story is *money.*

When you're up tight with worry, blood and juices don't flow freely; neither do thoughts. That's why public speaking instructors zero-in on speech anxiety. Tension inhibits personality. Until the speaker can relax his inner knowledge and better instincts are out of reach—as is his audience.

It's the same for the writer.

WHAT IS A WRITER?

A writer is
a reader,
a thinker,
a searcher,
a sleuth,
learning.
growing,
building
from youth,
by gradual
inception,
by aging,
progressing
unto the
perception
of truth.

TAKE THE SOLID STEPS

"I am the master of my fate." "Sail on, sail on!" "Yes, I can…"

We were all spoon-fed these mental vitamins as a child. From first grade our teachers ply us with motivational poetry and can-do stories to jump-start a desire for accomplishment. In high school and college we are exposed to the lives and quotes of the great. Then in business it's company publications chock full of incentive epigrams and sell yourself/sell the product articles. Specialty colleges hawk short-cut courses to riches on TV. And independent sellers pitch cleverly packaged "formula" seminars at resorts, hotels, and on cruise ships.

Today it's a quick-learn for everything— success guaranteed.

No wonder failure prevails. Not trained to give, we don't expect to exchange time and effort for our dream. We'd rather take a shot in the arm to become what we want to be instantly.

But writers don't *become* quickly.

In the beginning we may try the quickie courses and short-cut formulas; but if we shoot to the top without experience, it's a fluke. With rare exception the beginner sensation converts to a one-book has been. Sooner or later we discover the value of the slow teacher—trial and error. By learning what not to do, and what is vital not to forget, we progress. Mistakes jolt us to paying closer attention. Practice hones our talent. By repetition we gain confidence. Thus, from the first submission (accepted or rejected) a novice works up to professional. As Richard Bach of *Jonathan Livingston Segull* fame put it, "A professional writer is an amateur who didn't quit."

Punch-word reminders may prod you. A clever slogan can trigger your conscience, bolster your confidence, temporarily convince you that you'll win; but only the day after day grind makes it possible.

"It Is Possible" was the title of the winning presentation in a Toastmasters International Speech Contest. And the selected speaker convinced his audience there was miraculous power in his three-word formula for success: Desire, Action, and Persistence.

The key speaker at a recent writing seminar also touted a three-word sure-success formula. But he emphasized just one important factor, one the Toastmasters speaker left out. Prepare, Prepare, Prepare.

Another authority, writing in an old *Writer's Handbook* claimed "The three Ps of success are Practice, Persistence and Professionalism."

But should it be possible that any formula can generate winning power, I believe it would take four words, the proven requisites for success in any venture: Plan, Prepare, Proceed, Persist. All the well-paid, well-known writers I know took these solid steps in turn—and paid the full time/patience price to reach the heights. Don't skip any of them.

Plan. The first step toward winning is deciding where you want to go, which peak you are aiming for. And the second is picking a path. Sir William Osler said, "When plans are laid out in advance it is surprising how often circumstances fit in with them."

Make your plan, then start at the bottom and methodically climb toward your goal, not missing any steps. From letters to the editor, anecdotes, and fillers you graduate to short articles, profiles, how-to's, features, short stories … and on up, insuring these side paths converge on the highway to your goal. Does the house press of these magazines also publish books? Does the magazine you target for poetry print chapbooks and anthologies? Outline a route that will build, and keep leading you further.

Also, prepare a contingency plan.

For climbing conditions change; trends turn; magazines fold; editors move on. Anticipate such disappointments, as well as monotony, down-days, off-days, criticism, rejection ... Sooner or later all of these bandits will assault you. Consider in advance how you will resist them.

Prepare. Read, research, take specific courses, attend seminars, join an association of writers. Brush up on the techniques of commercial writing (as opposed to English composition). Learn the language of the business, the tricks of the trade. And last but not least, master manuscript mechanics (not to appear an amateur). Insure that editors will read your submissions. In *Getting Published* senior editors tell us they "don't bother to read improperly prepared manuscripts."

As part of a complete preparation also line up some support. Find a helpful librarian, make writer friends, subscribe to a good informative writer's magazine. You must be a loner while learning to write; but there comes a time to learn networking. Nobody becomes published alone.

You have a plan, you're prepared, you've lined up a support team, now immediately go into gear.

Proceed. From the moment of inspiration through R & D (research and development) you've been concentrating, but doing elementary work. Now you graduate to something harder. It isn't easy to recognize the right time to quit studying, planning, preparing, and start. But it's better to dive in sooner than later, for writing is self-teaching. Forge ahead; dare to go out on a limb. You want the best fruit; that's where the best fruit is.

Don't stop to analyze, wonder if it's safe, or go back and review. Just proceed, get some thoughts down on paper. Never mind striving for perfection. At the beginning that's procrastination in its most deadly form. Just keep moving and improving gradually. Of course you won't ignore an inspiration to make it better; but pleased with the effort or not, keep writing until you finish something. At this point the muse may speak to you but no supervisor will prod you; no one will nag you to produce. No one else is involved. It's up to you to proceed, and keep going.

Persist. Perseverance appears in nine out of ten achievement slogans. Henry Wadsworth Longfellow considered it the greatest element of success. He said, "knock long enough and loud enough, and you're sure to wake up somebody." Michael Blake wrote twenty screenplays (in twenty-five years) before he woke up a producer with *Dances With Wolves.*

All writers who have it made will tell you that "hanging in there" is the key requisite for success—also the hardest part. But after roughing it for ten years going on twenty you become conditioned. You'll keep climbing. Then, one day you'll be telling *your* never-quit story to the novices.

How long before that happens? I can't tell you. No one can. Doctors know in advance that they must complete a full traditional schedule before the money comes in. Lawyers can also determine the number of years in preparation. Writers chance a lifetime—but true to the motivators, we master our ultimate fate.

'TIS GIVEN

To the writer
with a desire
to serve,
'tis given—
the talent gift
from heaven,
and somehow,
somewhere
the chance to
develop it.

For the resolute,
somehow
there is time;
for the ready,
somewhere
opportunity.

THE PERFECT WRITER

Have you ever heard of the perfect writer?

No, I'm not talking about a computer software program, but a person, a writer who developed an expertise that almost defied description, a man who wrote to the heart and "...always with such perfect clarity, purity and understanding."

Francis Bonaventure de Sales.

Deemed a "perfect writer," this sixteenth-century religious thinker made an indelible mark on the minds of his time. And his eloquent French pen inspired posterity. Centuries later, in 1925, Pope Pious XI declared him "The Heavenly Patron Saint of All Writers." Today the likeness of St. Francis de Sales adorns the masthead of many writers' newsletters. Yet few of us know little if anything about him—some so little as to assume that "de sales" pertains to the selling of writing.

Born of nobility in 1567, Francis of the chateau de Sales, Louvre, France, became a "devout and eloquent preacher," and writing brilliantly, passed on invaluable insights for living.

So perfectly penned was *Introduction To A Devout Life* (a fount of timeless wisdom written for ordinary people) his superiors advised him not to write another book, because he "could never reach such perfection again." But he did, again and again, penning volumes of philosophy and wisdom acquired of patient study. The well known quote, "The more you say the less people will remember" is attributed to him. In quality and quantity the little-known Francis exceeded his contemporary, Shakespeare. And, reportedly, twenty-six thick volumes survive today. But how many moderns have read Francis Bonaventure de Sales? Have you?

I remember a well-published author saying (in *Writer's Digest*) that he had *just* discovered "writers have their own patron saint." For I too learned it late, and could hardly wait to read those "exquisite" writings. I've yet to find any. To this day I have not read any of Sales' original work. However, from encyclopedia sources, biographical information and quotes—from out of the past—the writer who some say achieved perfection, teaches me. The most invaluable lesson (probably the best advice ever given serious writers)—that practice with *patience* makes perfect. He also said, "Be patient with everyone, but above all with yourself."

Sometimes new writers overly anxious to publish will push, fret, try this, try that … and when a peer celebrates a sale, almost explode with envy. If that description fits, you might be on your way to burnout. Stop straining. Slow down. Take time to enjoy your writing, and notice how it improves.

It has been said that perfectionism is "paralysis by analysis." Straining for flawless performance in any endeavor, like haste makes waste, rarely improves the output, and often blocks progress.

Perfection is impossible. But striving toward quality is admirable. And the closer you get the happier the climbing. Progress exhilarates more than sitting on top counting your money; accomplishment gratifies more than notoriety. Treat yourself to the enjoyment of writing better every day, and the rewards will follow. According to the patron saint of writing, who lived the give and receive philosophy, "We give ourselves the best gifts."

Be generous with yourself. Don't withhold the best remuneration your chosen occupation has to offer. Realize that beside self-satisfaction everything pales.

When you attain heartfelt accomplishment, then you're ready to challenge that holdout publisher with work of quality. Submit naught but your best to anybody; and soon the law of nature will take over. Cream always rises to the top. Your cream may not come up to exquisite; you won't quite reach the honor of your picture as a logo; but you will shine as a writer. And is there any other star you'd rather reach for?

In our dreams, writing well and selling for top money balance out, but not in reality. The scale soon tips to the joy of creation *or* the pursuit of money. Every writer sooner or later makes that decision. Those tipped to creativity are well paid, though in different currency. The greatest rewards for a writer are pride and satisfaction—and thoroughly enjoying the striving.

This is not to suggest that it's necessary to settle for second best, or second money, to enjoy your writing, just that you don't relinquish the pleasure of creating by straining for perfection, because you won't reach it. Mortals never do.

You will not become a perfect writer.

But you will reach your goal, and enjoy the undertaking, if you listen to the one who came closest.

"Be patient…"

THE PINNACLE

Day after doggerel day
I climb,
sled-dog slow,
year after year
building up time;
and although
many a craggy
cliff I conquer,
still I bleed
below the line
electric-charged against
my need.

A rainbow
inaccessibility
glory fringed above the crowds,
success plays hide and seek
with me (the arc of promise
always partially hidden).

When will fate part
the clouds?

EXCELLENCE VERSUS PERFECTION

"Nobody is perfect ... everybody makes mistakes ... to err is human." In this enterprising century such time worn excuses are still being used, and accepted, for human performance.

In school we learn that 100 percent is not necessary; 70 percent is passing. This attitude carries over to the job. An employer gets only about 70 percent from the average employee. And the exceptions, the rare few that do strive for defectless results, are seldom commended. Why? Because such action, being a deviation from the norm, makes bosses apprehensive and coworkers resentful.

But suppose it were the other way around, mistakes becoming the rarity instead of the standard by which one qualifies for the human race? By widespread flawless accomplishment would we zoom to prosperity?

Yes of course, everyone *thought.*

This concept was once publicly promoted and put to the test. In "The Great Society" proposed by President Johnson the country's leaders were inspired. They would convince the workers to be "more concerned with the quality of their goals than the quantity of their goods." To implement this revolutionary concept of personal pride in accomplishment (and reinstate the word *quality* in America's vocabulary) a nationwide effort to promote perfection in the work place was initiated. In order to advance the quality of society it was necessary to advance the quality of individual contribution.

"There are no economical errors" became the slogan." At the onset of the space program it had become vital that errors be prevented. Detection finds them too late. The proverbial ounce of prevention could no longer be measured against a pound of cure, even a ton of cure. It was now priceless. The astronaut a million miles from earth couldn't afford that one diminutive error some assembly-line worker may allow himself.

Thus, **The Zero Defects Program** was born.

Endorsed by the U. S. Department of Defense, it forced both government and private industry to re-appraise old standards. Nationwide, Zero Defect seminars became mandatory, not only for the civil service but top management representatives of industry, and all government contractors.

And the results?

The Martin-Marietta Company of Florida, initiating the program for error free production on their Pershing Missile system, reported astounding success. As did General Electric's Flight Propulsion Division, Litton Industries, Thiokol Chemical, plus the entire automotive industry. By promoting flawless performance, rather than relying on detection and correction, thousands of organizations saved billions. And in reporting the phenomenon, the media pulled out all the stops.

I specifically remember this newspaper headline in enlarged, bold letters: "Perhaps the greatest money saving concept in history!" It prompted me to write an article on the subject-- my first attempt for *commercial* publication. Previously, I'd written only for The Government. But so popular was the subject, it won a prize in the annual *Writer's Digest* article contest, and later became a cover feature for *Success Unlimited* magazine.

Now, fifty years down the line, what has happened to the idea? Why are we not all still working like an army of ants (in our respective vocations) in pursuit of perfection? Why don't we hear anything about The Zero Defects Program today?

Because, ultimately, it had to be admitted that for fallible human beings perfect is not possible—or practical. Less than a year into the program executives of companies on the cutting edge of economic competition (where the most initial progress was made) found that production was being curtailed by the intense concentration on perfection. In myriad instances, it was concluded that "the perfectionism craze was cramping creative muscles and blocking imagination."

As it certainly does for writers. In all of the creative arts a surging idea permanently frozen into exactness ceases to soar, or even grow. Self-hobbled with perfectionism nose to the grindstone, we miss the wider horizon of improvement by inspiration.

With this conclusion corroborated, the better answer for company executives to the cry for improvement became "Total Quality Management" by dedication to excellence and efficiency. Adopting a gradual, continual reach for error-free performance (and advocating team effort) they found worked better with human nature. Now the slogan, "*excellence* as the norm not the exception", became official. The Zero Defects Program was dropped.

Although some people, equating perfection with virtue, still harbor an inherent desire to be perfect in all they do, most believe there is something fundamentally wrong with straining toward an unnatural condition. While the rest of the population fall somewhere in between.

As a motivated writer, wherever you fall, you can be caught in an inspiration/restriction compromise. Writers bound by the restrictive details dictated by editors and publishers, irrespective of talent and proficiency, all work under this pressure. In order to see our creations in print we must conform to industry regulation, as well as slant, style, length, voice, tone of the aimed-for publication, and the editor's personal preferences. In all these things, correctness is demanded. But in composition (not agreed upon) nothing is mandatory. And the minute errors that creep in are generally ignored.

What a day it would be if total war had been declared on error, and continued. Today we might see "Made in America" plastered proudly on every manufactured work and everything else created in this country. American authors might be winning all the literary prizes! But that's far from likely. Conventional thought patterns are not easily changed.

So what is the highest middle ground—the most profitable response to a burning literary ambition?

Experts advise approaching each project with unbridled imagination and calm precision, believing that every article, story, or poem can be improved--and gradually improving day by day, with an eye on excellence.

In the wisdom of Aristotle, "Excellence is not an art but a habit." By a conscientious climb we can attain it; while perfect lies forever out of reach. Perfection has been proven "a mean form of idealism." In *Bird by Bird: Some Instructions on Writing and Life,* author Anne Lamott reiterates, "it cramps our mental muscles … keeps us writing in tight, worried ways."

If you're up tight, relax. Always do your best; but remember "To err is human." None of your competitors will reach perfection either. We all make fewer mistakes when we don't strain for the impossible.

Excellence versus perfection … Excellence wins.

ENDLESS DECISION

After the inspiration,
the imagining,
phrasing,
polishing …
living with
the inner terror
(lest the seed not
grow to blossom
in all its beauty),
we wrestle with the
endless decision:

Retain the creation,
lovingly,
endlessly
checking,
trimming
(in pursuit
of perfection)?
or fearfully
send it forth
to bleed on
the barbs of
repeated rejection?

HITTING THE TARGET

Beginning writers share a common dream—breaking into print. Once they break the barrier…!

Don't you believe it. Hitting the target *isn't* always easier thereafter. In most cases, whether or not you've been published before is immaterial. You win when you send your well-written article or story to the right editor at the right time. You see your work in print regularly when you become as proficient at selling as you are at writing.

Yet this business aspect is often sorely neglected in a writer's training. Teachers teach writing. Experts spur beginners with quips like, "just write, and send it in." Mentors encourage them to keep trying, and develop a thick skin against editor opposition (rejection). But rarely do they receive tips on how to ascertain the editor who won't resist.

Taking a chance on a novice writer sometimes requires as much courage on the part of the editor as it does for you to make those first submissions. The editor may be new too; and required to answer to the publisher for her mistakes, could be as nervous as you are. On the other hand, an experienced editor seeing potential in your work, but recognizing that you are not quite ready, might offer helpful advice-- or not bother. Editors are people with different personalities, different backgrounds, and different degrees of expertise.

But such things may not enter the beginner's mind. After studying, and practicing for maybe years, they enter publishing territory naively thinking they're past the hard part. Then discovering all that is involved in marketing their work, all they still don't know... many flounder, and carelessly shoot at the first target.

"Don't let your dream lay in the drawer" may be good advice; but also remember, "fools rush in." After robbing your consciousness of every drop of inspiration to scratch the surface of truth on a subject that inspired you, after laboring over the writing to make it the best you could, do take time to select a market that *possibly* will be receptive. Don't blindly send it in.

The most common complaint among editors is that writers don't study their publication before submitting. "Most of them don't even know what we're about," an editor friend told me. "It's as if they have no idea who our readers are." And she claims it isn't only the novices.

Writers at all levels spend too little time on market research. Late beginners (after shelving their dream for years while raising a family, or enduring a dead-end job to support one) resent giving up their hard-acquired writing time for *anything or* simply believe "if it's good it will sell." Others who were lucky early justify their haphazard study with an "I did it before" over-confidence.

When the first article I wrote for commercial publication was published and I received a substantial check—while working overtime on a special writing project for The Government (without remuneration). I thought, when I retire and can freelance full-time I'll be in the money!

I was naïve. Years of more rejections than acceptances educated me. That first time I had simply blundered upon the right publication. Not until I buckled down and seriously concentrated on matching manuscript to market, did I start selling regularly. Then I learned that "selling" doesn't always mean money. In the writing game, generally, it means acceptance. You may be paid in courtesy copies and a byline. But as your publishing education progresses you discover that bylines build to money. When your work is published your name becomes familiar to editors; and down the line you might be offered paying assignments. We learn by trial and error; and we shorten our apprenticeship when we learn the whole business.

After becoming an accomplished writer you must develop proficiency as an editor, secretary, salesperson, promoter/publicist, time management specialist, and most important, a full-time researcher.

How diligently do you search, and research, to find your markets?

Do you look everywhere? If you limit your search to *The Writer's Market* and market sections of writer's magazines, you are restricting your chances. For little known, less advertised, and unadvertised publications, look in university and company libraries. There are myriad magazines you won't see in Daltons, the drug store, or city libraries. And hundreds of them are not listed in *Writer's Market.* So don't be above scavenging. Pick up discarded newsletters, leaflets, religious publications, on a bus, in the post office, or blowing in the street. What some of them print may surprise you.

A check of newsstands will reveal some national, wide circulation magazines that do not solicit submissions from freelance writers. Many have a stable of reliable regulars and don't want the extra work an avalanche of mail will bring. Others periodically pull their listings when they have a backlog. However, now and then one of these top magazines will surprise you, and solicit submissions.

Suppose you read in *The Writer* or *Writer's Digest* that a well-known slick magazine is inviting unknowns to submit. They have a new editor. He knows there is unrecognized talent out there, and wants to give you a break; once he walked the lonely road. A dream come true, you think. Think again. Thousands of fellow strugglers (and established writers who haven't made a sale lately) are going to read that same article, and think the same thing.

That isn't opportunity; it's enhanced competition.

Back when you made the big decision to live a literary life, you knew there'd be keen competition. As a practicing writer you discover it gets keener and keener. Prepare yourself; learn all you can. The more you know the more times you win--although sometimes after thorough study you still miss the target completely.

There will be occasions when you think a psychic could not have foreseen a rejection. As French author André Maurois said, "In literature as in love we are often astonished at what is chosen by others." But with concerted effort you *can* reduce disappointments.

Start hitting the target more often.

BLOOD SISTERS

Success and failure,
like love and hate, are
closer than you think.

Together they hover
round every gate,
balanced on the brink
of inclination,
awaiting decision.

But fate is not sealed
by any one action;
blood-tied opposites
are interchangeable.

The bright one
never final;
the dark one
never fatal.

IMAGINATIVE MARKETING

Most writers recognize, and utilize, the power of imagination for the creative side of the writing business, but not for the necessary next step--the marketing of their creations. How about you? Do you approach the job reluctantly, resenting the time it takes from your writing—and then wonder why you are not selling?

No wonder. Without enthusiasm we seldom succeed.

It is imperative that we change our thinking; and make marketing interesting. Pre-labeled a "dullsville" job, the selling of what we create is often approached haphazardly. Or put off indefinitely.

But should we consider it a search for treasure…

New writers, who don't receive assignments, must start their search for markets cold. And alone. But it should be with anticipation, and imagination. Learn to apply the law of expectancy. Envision your piece accepted by every editor whose criteria it meets—and insure that it does. Play the what-if game. What if this magazine buys it? Maybe it's good enough for that better paying one. What if both editors like it!

While the professional may consider it a cardinal sin to write anything without a market in mind, for the novice this is not yet possible. The beginner (and the genius) dream, pour their hearts out on paper, and think business later.

But the minute the piece is finished, and polished, you've dreamed long enough. Now you must enter unknown territory. Time to buy a map, research, and prepare to explore every potential area. Unearth all the facts; dig deep, like the prospector who knows the gold is there-- as is your treasure. Learn to recognize landmarks, read between the lines. And if you can, discuss possibles with other writers. Brainstorm.

Brainstorming, according to my dictionary, is "a method of attacking problems by intense discussion and spontaneous idea swapping..." The procedure can also be effective within one mind—between the conscious and the subconscious. Feed your subconscious detailed information as well as ideas. They will churn together and later surface to help you determine a "likely," which you will study further. Possibility after possibility, weighing new factors, you will see something pertinent you missed before.

You might reconsider the magazine you saw yesterday in the doctor's office, or that new one you read but couldn't find in any market listing. Soon your mind whirs with images of possible customers--like the dream you had when you first began writing it. Dream on.

Picture the layout of your article or story in print. Imagine the title on the cover. Conjure up readers engrossed in it, maybe responding! Harness the power of imagination for double duty; and you'll enjoy the selling as you did the writing.

Also have fun analyzing your story. Is it about computers, politics, children, gambling...? Consider the regional aspects: country, city, climate, family situation—every possible tie-in for reader identification. Or change them if feasible.

When we brand marketing a dull job that fate forces upon us (if we want to see our creation in print) we tend to go at it mechanically. But mechanics and the practical rules only count when you submit to a fitting publication; and good writing speaks for you, only to the *right* editor. Use the power of imagination to find them both.

Perhaps you never thought of using imagination for pragmatical problems; but when you do the picture changes, as does your attitude. Any action wholly based on fact, rules and regulation becomes boring--because we are restricted to the known. But soaring into the unknown, imagining and dreaming, opens up the higher field, the one without boundaries.

Next time you finish something you've been working on for months (and dreaming of selling) try to think of your market search as an exciting hunting trip. Like the big-game hunter, fully prepare yourself before the venture; determine exactly what you are looking for; then stride out confidently with alert eye.

And should such a trip return no spoils, what does the disappointed sportsman do? He reviews every turn he took, every unnecessary noise he made, every near-miss shot—and psychically sees that perfect buck in his sights next time.

The treasure hunter also uses this trick of mind-picturing a success to become a reality. Propelled by imagination into one dangerous adventure after another, mentally seeing the buried gold or crusted box of jewels in a sunken ship (and the money they translate to) gives full imaginative power to search after search after search.

How many writers search so intensely for their treasure? Certainly, we dream as much, and thrill at the support of imaginative power when we're creating. So why do we not recruit it to help us sell what we create?

From an article in *The Wall Street Journal:* "Freelancers get paid absolutely zero if they do not produce." That's only half the story. We can produce reams and still get paid zero, until we master the art of selling what we write.

If you are having trouble selling, try imaginative marketing.

BECOMING AN AUTHOR

For a paragraph
in the local paper,
your face on TV,
an inch or two on the
library shelf, you seal
yourself in a cell
of solitude,
deny your eyes
the beauty of nature:
sunset, sunrise,
sprays of silver
o'er rippling cobalt--
even the pure azure
that lovers see ...

Oh how austerely
we regiment
our short allotted days,
all for that temporary
season of praise.
Author, author!

THE PART THAT LUCK PLAYS

Every writer dreams of winning a literary competition.

When luck grants you *first place,* or any coveted award, it's a boost up the ladder. The gate to recognition swings open. You experience the elation of peer envy. Your name becomes familiar to editors, who begin to look upon your work with favor. And if you take home a prestigious prize the ensuing parade of publicity almost guarantees acceptance thereafter.

No wonder freelancers are tempted to gamble—no matter how long the shot. But we shouldn't be tempted too often.

Publicized competition stretches us, sharpens our abilities; we push harder and polish more than for regular submissions. And that's good as a periodic tonic; sometimes we get sluggish. On the other hand there's danger in habitually entering contests, if that extra effort breaks out in a rash of anxiety and we begin shooting wildly. Like the get-rich-quick hold on the gambler, the dreamer-writer catches contest fever. I know more than a few who suffer the malady—good, hard working writers going broke on contest fees. They wouldn't think of paying to be published, but they repeatedly pay not to be.

Taking chances is the name of the writing game; but continually entering contests is like sending a reading fee for every submission. And as the fever rises, you start ignoring the odds, and daring out of your league. Entering contests can be an exiting change, or an expensive invitation to disappointment. If you like to enter contests now and then, select them carefully. Nothing is gained by attempting to lasso a prize beyond your reach. Unless your experience and qualifications fit the criterion your chances of winning equate to catching a feather in the wind.

And think of the precious time that's lost.

Of the thousands of literary contests, perhaps hundreds will fit your expertise and ability. But unless you ferret out those only you waste your time. Thoroughly research and evaluate the level of competition *before* taking the chance. Don't bruise your own ego by stretching for the wrong brass ring.

In this speculative profession we must risk rejection and failure to progress. To make anything like a salary we must continually play the dice game--pitch and hope, pitch and hope … But every throw, we should know what we're doing. No one wins with a wild one. A novice doesn't send to *The New Yorker,* and beginners don't compete in contests for seasoned professionals. Until your talent is honed, be patient. Don't squander your time and money for the privilege to jump and fall short.

Unlike the lottery, top prize in a literary competition cannot be won by *anybody.* The "lucky" first had to qualify. If you doubt this, a background check of the big money winners will reveal convincing evidence that the prize was earned by hard work and experience. With rare exceptions, the winner is one who climbed up the ladder to media attention, invitations to speak at seminars, and the lucrative offers that follows such a win.

If you want to try for booty in contest competition, make it a race you can win. There are contests for every level of experience and expertise. The annual *Writer's Market* alone publishes nearly sixty pages of Contest and Awards, each category conveniently arranged according to the kind of writing you do, nonfiction, fiction, poetry, script writing, journalism, etc.

Make your selections by category, subject, and area of expertise; then write for details, rules and restrictions. And check periodicals for *updated* information on the contests you are considering. Writing magazines also publish newly announced competitions. And for a nominal fee you can buy *Grants and Awards Available to American Writers.* The latest edition claimed, "...thirty-two additional pages of listings for writers of every genre, for writers everywhere in the country."

The first contests you enter, offering only publicity or five or ten dollars to the winner, will be easy. Then with the boost a win gives to your confidence you can gradually work up to $100, $500, $1000 (and countless other amounts) all the way to "The Nobel" million.

To find out what a certain contest is currently paying, go to the Internet: www.LiteratureAwards.com.

Perhaps you'll be surprised to discover that the award most writers covet pays very little (comparatively)—but <u>the</u> prize (The Pulitzer) boosts them higher in the eyes of their peers, and the public.

`There's something about The Pulitzer. It pays only $5000; but it's like the literary Oscar.

People forget the "Nobel" victors, but not the Pulitzer Prize winners. The following authors won more than a decade ago, and all are still enjoying popularity.

For fiction: James A, Michener, Harper Lee, Norman Mailer, and Alice Walker. For nonfiction: Carl Sagan, Theodore White, Barbara Tuchman, and Studs Terkle. For poetry: Robert Lowell, Robert Frost, Marianne Moore, and Galway Kinnel. By winning The Pulitzer these lucky authors became household names.

When Annie Dillard won, for *Pilgrim at Tinker Creek,* few people outside the literary community had heard of her. A few months later we saw her name everywhere. Archibald MacLeish, a three-time winner, credits The Pulitzer for his success in several fields other than writing and poetry. Anna Quindlen, a winner for her column in *The New York Times,* soon had columns in magazines and newspapers across the country.

Advantage, privilege, prestige, the title "famous author"… the most popular prize promotes a writer's career like no other. Less money up front translates to more later. The Pulitzer is gold.

Yet, surprisingly, the contest has few restrictions.

Founder Joseph Pulitzer's only stipulation; "For various accomplishments, achievement, and forms of excellence," leaves the door wide open. Winning subjects have run the gamut from accounts of the atomic bomb to animals in a cave; from international intrigue to small town problems; from the birth of a baby to the death of a diplomat. And, since only individual excellence wins, the prize board will accept informal nominations and direct applications from unlimited sources, including the author, or any reader. Little known to the general public several submissions by readers (and authors) have won.

It is entirely possible that you might one-day win.

To start working up to it, compete in your own league, follow the rules **exactly,** and send your very best.

In "Advice to the Prizelorn," an article published in *Poets and Writers* Magazine, writing judge Nancy Mairs said, "Winning a contest transformed my professional life." Not long after, she was judging contests.

Today she reads entries that lack the precepts of good writing with exasperation, and mentally counsels the anonymous writers. "I'm on your side. I want you to win. But you have a few responsibilities." Basically, know the rules (because she must abide by them); know your craft (others entering the competition will); and know the risk (the part that luck plays).

As a contest judge Mairs takes her responsibility seriously. She reminds contestants that "only one entry can win," that "judges are people" with different backgrounds and interpretations; and she clearly states the odds. "There are always a number of talented losers who did everything right. It comes down to my decision."

Whenever you enter a contest remember these things. And keep in mind that your chance is born of all that went before. Luck plays but a bit part; it's only on stage that one last hour.

VOCATIONS OF VALUE

Working the mind,
filtering truths
(old as eternity),
presenting them
redefined for
a new century,
is the mission
of the writer,
the poet,
novelist,
journalist,
biographer...

Every literary
endeavor, a
contribution
to society.

THE RIGHT TO READ

Did you know The Bill of Rights does not give us the right to read anything we want? The first amendment (freedom of speech, and of the press) doesn't address the reading of free speech. It's an assumed freedom.

But can everybody read anything you write?

The U. S. Government rarely bans books. However, at lower levels of officialdom book banning is common practice. Despite the advisory service of the Office of Intellectual Freedom, and the work of The Freedom to Read Foundation, we have actual and potential intellectual freedom problems. All across this country, behind the closed doors of community councils and local school boards, conspiracies flourish against the freedom to read what we choose.

In this land of freedom of expression there's little tolerance by local big brother officials for what they might consider "detestable." *Free Speech For Me—But Not For Thee* (By Nat Hentoff).

These self-appointed guardians of good (with diversified ideas of what good is) search for reasons (supported by particular religious or moral systems) to prevent the public from reading your books—when they don't like your ideas. In the land of liberty this must be unconstitutional.

Supreme Court Justice Louis D. Brandeis once called the practice "insidious encroachments by men of zeal, well-meaning but without understanding…and one of the greatest dangers to liberty."

Echoing this thought, The Office for Intellectual Freedom, The American Library Association, and several other literary organizations, together with authors' societies and college and university presses, sponsor Banned Book Week. This annual effort to awaken the American public to the ongoing suppression of their freedom to read is enthusiastically supported by myriad independent and national bookstores. And by authors who have been ostracized by opinion.

Bookstore managers display, and make available to the public, long annotated lists of all the books that have ever been banned, anywhere. They schedule banned book readings. One local store distributes copies of The First Amendment. Other sellers (and lenders) of the written word set up impressive displays of the better known formerly banned, or destroyed books that later became holy wisdom, educational authority, or classics.

The Holy Bible is the best example. Martin Luther's translation was burned. The Revised Standard Version experienced the wrath of the Fundamentalists. Ethiopia once banned all versions. In 1986, all recent translations were banned in Turkey.

The Ill-fated classics include *The Diary of Ann Frank, Alice's Adventures In Wonderland, The Adventures of Huckleberry Finn,* even *The American Heritage Dictionary* (for objectionable language).

And surely listed, if not displayed, are some favorites that opened your eyes--all bearing testimony to an ignorant age failing to recognize genius ahead of its time. The most common subject offenders include war, religion, and fear of influence against the prevailing power. Some examples you may remember: Upton Sinclair's *The Jungle*, banned by The Communists; Jack

London's *Call Of the Wild*, burned by The Nazis; *All Quiet On the Western Front*, forbidden to Austrian soldiers, and barred from the Czech military.

The United States of America (The Freedom Nation) bans fewer books than other countries; but "we the people" have no guarantee. One administration tried to ban *The CIA and the Cult of Intelligence* while still in manuscript form. Remember that national controversy? It turned into a media hey-day. Ultimately the masses rose up screaming for their right to know--their right to read.

Not long thereafter the noose on this illegally constricted freedom began loosening. In a democracy complete suppression of thoughts and ideas contrary to the will of the leaders is not possible. No matter how much propaganda the people are fed, they are not all taken in. All the scattered fires of new and different thinking cannot be smothered. In a country without royalty or a dictator, even at top popularity the leader must bow to the built-in controls of the constitution. The radicals must be heard. There's no way to conceal thoughts by repressing evidence that they exist. The wildest ideas from the least educated laymen go in the pot from which "justice for all" is ladled.

Thus, by battle of minds this country progresses toward the dreamed of ideal--true democracy, though it still be far in the future. Justice Hugo Black, commenting on a layman's view of The First Amendment, revealed the disparity yet to be legally compromised.

"What he likes is constitutional, and that which he doesn't like is unconstitutional."

In the interim, the lesser officials, continue to ban books with a vengeance—all kinds of books for all kinds of reasons. It seems as if these self-appointed big brothers think the people are in danger of being run over by ruthless minds. They censor by ignorance, fear, taboos, and traditions, rarely taking into account that mores and morals change.

Considering the accepted moral standard of the time, in these famous cases (*Lady Chatterley's Lover, Ulysses,* and *Tropic of Cancer)* censoring made a degree of sense. But in light of modern mores, these recent restrictions do not.

In 1993 a children's book was banned in Maryland because "the mother in the story was considered neglectful." In California a book of riddles was removed from an elementary school because "it is demeaning to those unable to figure out the answers." A local library justified expurgating from a picture book the sketch of a nude boy, "nude for no reason." Even a fantasy was banned, "for integrationist propaganda" (a black and a white rabbit got married).

And remember the yo-yo banning of *Working* by Studs Terkel? When first published the book was banned by many public schools; later it became required reading, only to be banned again.

If this trend of banning running wild is not officially curbed some of your writing (whatever you write) could suffer public censure. It might be blocked by an opinionated publisher, or burned by a self-appointed big brother. Some worry that "Down the road these fanatics might try to dictate what we can write too."

Because of uncontrolled power over diverse opinion, the world suffers the loss of many invaluable books by the greatest minds, i.e. Aristotle's historical account of the eighteen republics that existed before his time, the writings of Cicero on early government, the fifty gospels condemned as "spurious" by a Pope—all burned.

In our time, banning instead of burning (outright destruction) does indicate progress. But still, in the twenty-first century, citizens of "The Freedom Nation" should be free to read everything The First Amendment allows to be written, and published. Toward that end, every

September The American Library Association, with full support of the media, endeavors to draw attention to the practice of behind-the-scenes censorship.

On Banned Book Week lists this year are best selling children's books (The Harry Potter series), and several past year offenders. *The Chocolate War, Fallen Angels, The Color Purple,* and *I Know Why the Caged Bird Sings.* When the story about a boy in a Catholic school who refuses to sell school candy (*The Chocolate War*) was published in 1974, the author expected it to be banned--for four letter words and sex talk. But now he strongly maintains it doesn't warrant negative attention. Twenty-seven years later, in a review for *Book World,* Robert Cormier said,"Kids these days know they are not living in a fairy-tale kind of land."

How long will this unofficial literary censure be allowed?

There is no prediction. But for more detailed information about Banned Book Week, and how you as a concerned writer can help insure the freedom to read, contact the Office of Intellectual Freedom (OIF), Washington, D. C. 800-545-2433, ext. 4220.

PROGRESS

Out of the night
literature was born,
then progress
(blind humanity
seeing the light).

By dint of writing,
earthly sojourners
slowly learning--
ending the fight.

STEERING CLEAR OF PLAGIARISM

*"O'er his books his eyes began to roll
in pleasing memory of all he stole."*
> --Alexander Pope.

Do you steal? Sometimes borrow from other writers without giving credit? No? You don't think so?

Only Adam could be *sure* no one said it before.

We all plagiarize, knowingly or unknowingly. Either we err or are deceived by careless research, misinterpretation, second-hand information ... Sometimes we credit quotes to the wrong writer—the one who formerly stole. Since "there's no new thing under the sun," honest originality may be plagiarism unidentified. It could be true that "all writers plunder the dead." Surely, some great authors have drawn from the well of previously generated literature without giving credit. Many have freely admitted it.

Milton wrote, *"Only if it be not bettered by the borrower, among good authors, is accounted plagiary."* Voltaire suggested that writers were misnamed. *"Call them bookmakers, not authors; range them rather among second-hand dealers."* According to Goethe (reportedly) there would be little left of him if he were to discard what he owed to others.

That all authors owe somebody is undeniable. The professionals, however, having ascertained the fine line that cuts off on the safe side of piracy, select more exclusively. But then again they sometimes risk it.

Perhaps you've heard F. Scott Fitzgerald's story. He felt safe using his wife's letters and diaries for *The Beautiful and The Damned.* Wives can't testify against their husbands. But when Zelda recognized several passages of her *exact wording* she angrily told reporters—and subsequently the world! The publicity and hyperbole that followed is said to have triggered the downfall of this great novelist.

"Plagiarism is using any material written or spoken by another person." This sounds black and white. However, you will discover that there are many other descriptions, in various shades of gray. This makes a writer of integrity nervous. You know that copying exactly is stealing; but according to *The Writer's Encyclopedia*, so is "closely imitating ...without permission, acknowledgment, or compensation." According to *A Handbook of Literature* (50th Anniversary Edition) theft of a detailed plot, used as new, is also plagiarism. By law an idea cannot be copyrighted, so cannot be stolen "... only the written expression of it." Yet Webster's dictionary tells us, "To plagiarize is to steal and use the *idea* or writings of another as one's own." And it's illegal use when what we take involves infringement of copyright. However, when it's in the public domain it is not illegal. But it is considered unethical. Even if you could remember all these different definitions, are they not somewhat contradictory?

So what do conscientious writers do?

We learn to paraphrase. Becoming proficient in paraphrasing may be the most profitable aspect of the writing game. But be careful. Blunder too close and you risk creating suspicion, especially among your more astute peers. A familiar phrase will prick the ear of a potential accuser; slather on butter to fatten your ideas and a law suite hovers. Even the stigma of *accusation* can be costly. Don't take chances.

Even practiced professionals sometimes get caught. Others get away with it.

According to *The Writer's Home Companion,* six years after a book came out by Sherwood Anderson (*Winesberg, Ohio*) a poem by Theodore Dreiser was published in a literary magazine containing almost an exact duplicate of one paragraph, but in poem format.

Writer taking from writer goes on, generation after generation—and has done since writing was invented. However, in ancient times it was not a sin, nor even a consideration. There being no publishing companies, or lawyers, it was common practice to take any story you liked and adapt it with new names and locations. Only later was censure of copied words attempted. But always the words of the writer have been disseminated to the world--by Roman runners, pony express, trucks, trains, planes, all the way to e-mail—with proliferation ever increasing. Surely, today *everything* has been written, and rewritten in every way.

To the wary beginner these are inhibiting thoughts. No wonder they hesitate to write for fear they might plagiarize, and procrastinate for fear their creations will be stolen. It's the most prevalent worry among student writers that editors, or somebody, will steal their ideas. And the common apprehension reaches plague proportions when they witness incidents that seem to offer proof. Like the following.

One day a woman stormed into writing class waving a magazine and shouting that an editor had rejected her article, and then published the essence of the piece, staff written. Slinging the magazine down on my desk she stabbed at the open page, and turned to face her classmates.

"And they tell us editors don't steal. All my ideas are in here!"

Coleridge once said, "The plagiarists are always suspicious of being stolen from." That may be true; but so are many honest insecure writers. Lost in a sea of conflicting information the conscientious novice wastes a lot of good writing time worrying about plagiarism.

I hope you won't allow this worry and suspicion to cripple your output. Believe me; unethical editors are extremely rare. After your work is published and out roaming for readers, yes, you're vulnerable; it is exposed to criticism by everybody, including unscrupulous competitors. But you needn't walk on eggs afraid to borrow anything. There are worry-free ways to incorporate second hand material.

Should you be unable to pin down the original source to credit, give anonymous credit. Or use vague attributions, i.e. someone once said; according to an expert, reportedly, it is generally believed.... Make up your own expressions. If the origin is not provable, present it (reworded) as material for thought, rather than fact. These are not illegal practices. When quoting a contemporary author always include the full name and the name and date of the publication. This not only foils eager-beaver critics, it clears you in case that writer misquoted, or wrongly claimed originality.

When facing the ogre of uncertainty regarding fair use, always remember that the less you take the safer. Pull only the essence. If it's a long quote chop it up; and use the most pertinent parts between ellipses. This concentrates the power of the message, and also adds interest to the page.

All above considered, you needn't worry about plagiarism. With accumulated experience, and a majority of the facts, your common sense will guide you. Just remember, to steer clear of plagiarism *never use as your own what you didn't write,* and borrow sparingly—and carefully label what you borrow.

Agreeing with Milton, Voltaire and Goethe, Emerson said, "A writer, having once shown himself capable of original writing is entitled thenceforth to steal from the writing of others, at discretion."

Discretion is the key.

SELF LECTURE

That "special" invaluable
talent seed,
the heavenly spark planted
within us,
like everything in embryo,
suffers need
of nurturing to spawn the
impetus …

My intrinsic artistic potential
must be developed,
or the gift is wasted --
for lack of confidence,
joy untasted.

For hesitance,
I miss my chance
to fly.

LATE GREAT LITERARY CAREERS

If you are late getting started on your writing career, whatever your age, don't think it's too late. Later can be better for a writer.

There's power in a creative restlessness that's been brewing for years. That fallow time was preparing you. And if you dare to leave the comfort of your accumulated knowledge to strike out one more time as an amateur (for another level of development) you have all it takes.

Aging doesn't automatically drain brainpower; even at 90 creativity doesn't necessarily ice-over. It depends on the will of the individual. And according to R. S. Zimmerman, Ph.D. (writing in *Modern Maturity*) "mentally active people show *much* slower rates of decline."

In an interview at 73 writer, composer, actor, musician, comedian, philosopher, Steve Allen (after 45 books and 42 albums) said he felt more creative than ever. "Obviously this is not true of my every human activity; I couldn't run the 100 meter dash as fast today as I did 40 years ago. But the creativity is still there ... creative people never retire."

They often doubt, however.

In one of my writing classes for seniors, a retired teacher who had shelved her desire to write for thirty years, suddenly exclaimed, "Oh, there's so much I don't know; and I have so little time left!"

TIME OUT. The rest of the session we talked about the *advantages* of a late writing career. Consider.

Unless the desire dies, older translates to greater potential. Live and learn. After years of straining toward understanding nature has filled in most of the general knowledge gaps. You've seen almost everything, and experienced every emotion. Most of you have learned time management (a most definite plus for a writer). This collective-living education easily counterbalances youth and a "writing" degree. Time tips the scale in your favor. As a senior you are capable, confident, seasoned, and in control. Those waiting years have transported you to the golden hour of vision, which is said to commence after fifty—the youth of old age.

It is in this second youth, loaded with experience and long-dammed desire, that we make the most progress. With myriad yesterdays to draw from, and having developed responsibility, patience, the power of concentration, we can't help but learn faster. The more sand dropped to the bottom of the hourglass the clearer we see is a documented fact; research proves that mature beginners publish sooner—and many reach distinction.

Daniel Defoe, pushing 60 before he was free to write, made it with his first novel. *Robinson Crusoe* became a classic. Harriet Doerr began at 65, "after a long journey with many detours." Starting with what she knew best, drawing on a lifetime of living and traveling in Mexico, she tried short stories. Three of them published in a literary journal won the Transatlantic Henfield Foundation Award, and became the basis of *Stones for Iberra*-- winner of the 1984 American Book Award for first fiction.

If, like these successful authors, you are past what is called the prime of your life, and have relegated your desire to the back burner for half a century, grab your belated opportunity and go. The light has finally turned green. Waste no more time lamenting; fate may not have cheated you. Consider this Mickey Spillane quote: "If you're a singer you lose your voice; a baseball player loses his arm, but a writer gets more knowledge."

For a writer, older is better in more ways than it is worse. In the writing business one rarely encounters age discrimination. Usually the editor doesn't even know your age; he may never see you; and it's not required that you divulge the information. But should you be pigeonholed in the "senior" category, today there are advantages. True, an agent may hesitate to take you on "because you don't have many productive years left." Some publishers may refuse to invest in you. Because, per *Publisher's Weekly,* "they believe it can be more difficult to launch older writers." But look at the plus side.

Since the early1990s publishing houses that cater to older writers have been springing up in surprising numbers.

Senior Press of Hilton Head Island, South Carolina, founded by a woman writer of 29 years experience (who sensed she was being rejected because of her age) is a good example. First she published her own book, then a novel by a California retiree, followed by the first fiction of a 78-year old journalist … This press publishes older writers exclusively.

And what about *"When I Am Old I Shall Wear Purple,"* published by Papier-Mache? Owned and edited by senior women, they "prefer receiving from older-women writers."

The number of book publishers catering to the mature beginner keeps growing. There's also a proliferating list of better magazines soliciting the work of seniors. Add to these pluses the good luck of electronic publishing exploding on the scene--opportunity for everybody—just when the time was right for you.

If writing is what you have always wanted to do, don't curb your creative energy any longer. Let others be deterred by the wind-down mentality of the majority. Statements like the following, made by a psychiatrist in a TV interview, may be true for many, but it doesn't fit you.

"After mid-life people are prone to drift. The over-50 consider the present but a time connector between past and future ... the senior mind seems to bend in that direction, as if they've wound up, and feel that the remaining time is of little value."

This is a generality statement. It doesn't apply to writers. Whatever the countdown, desire and determination will launch a writing career. And age is an added asset; Your mind is fully primed.

In his ninth decade, Nobel Prize Winner George Bernard Shaw said, "You imagine what you desire, will what you imagine, and create what you will, in time." Note the key phrase, in time. Shaw liked to tell about how time benefited him. You have probably heard this quote. "I offered my first book to every publisher on the English speaking earth; their refusals were unanimous. But fifty years later they clamored to publish anything that had my name on it."

The late bloom of William James' career is another example. Blessed with money, education, opportunity, family support (all the advantages a writer dreams of) still, he didn't publish until his profound thoughts were sufficiently ripened by time.

Read biography and you'll discover that most of the world's great writers were late beginners. Those who became your idols turned the universal age attitude inside out. They proved that there is no cut-off time for creativity—that later is better.

Fall is the writer's season.

A late great literary career *is* possible.

TO WORRIED WRITERS

Don't you believe
"a picture is worth
a thousand words;"
twenty well chosen,
(an artful description)
will wing the scene
closer to the heart.
Forget about
the new technology
threatening your career;
in every communication
is it not a writer's
words that are spoken?
And like Aladdin,
you have miracle tools
to open doors…
Worry not that speech
symbology will die,
still, society
demands hard copy.

WRITING CAREER EXTRAORDINAIRE

You have chosen a literary career. Writing is your life; you don't want to do anything else. But after years of study and practice you still don't hit the high paying markets. You barely make a living. Your career is going nowhere.

Time to face the ugly reality that the public judges talent by publicity and hype.

Mediocrity often hides behind a façade of fame. Marginal talent possessed of ego and ambition can soar to the pinnacle, while genius sweats in obscurity. If your name is in the paper, if you are interviewed on TV, if you hire a publicist or rigorously promote yourself, the world assumes that your talent is extraordinary, that you are accomplished and worthy, and the writers they don't hear about are not.

This general assumption dominates in every field of artistry. In entertainment for example.

Did you know that Bob Hope employed five publicists? Street smart and ambitious, this former vaudeville performer discerned early that it takes more than talent to win. By mastering the trickery of showmanship, and all the different media techniques, an actor of average ability became America's best-known, best-paid entertainer.

To outrun the competition Hope learned to capitalize on the power of publicity, and play to the heart of the majority. Performing for those in the news (away from home fighting for their country) bought free publicity by the landfall. The money automatically rolled in. Further capitalizing on this gold-mine situation, he took along his own cameras and recording equipment, thus making one performance do double duty-- and each showing on TV *monetarily* topping the original.

As every actor and singer knows (and writer soon learns) the number one criterion for making money is generating publicity, enough to put your name on the lips of every potential fan. That's how one of the best known poets became famous. Walt Whitman wrote his own reviews, and additionally, writing under assumed names, published numerous articles praising his own poetry.

Today, it takes self-generated publicity to sell a subsequent book for the "lucky" author soon forgotten. The initial promotion push by a publisher doesn't last long. Nothing beats making "the list," and the best-seller list is synonymous with success. Make it more than once and the world of material things is yours. However, for some, no amount of money is worth an effort that goes against their integrity.

If you are adverse to self-promotion there is another road to riches of another kind. Less hype, less glitter, and more satisfaction. On this alternate path promotion to fulfillment is by word-of-mouth. The golden ring is gratitude (which many covet more than money). After years of perfecting your craft, when you *know* how to write, if the rewards aren't coming you might consider the requiting career minus the compromise. As a writing instructor and mentor you'll bask in the gratification of helping others, and make a contribution to humanity.

You don't believe me?

Meet an extraordinary example. The late Phyllis Heald of Tucson, Arizona. You may not have heard her name; you've never seen her on TV. This prolific author, playwright, consultant, critic, and articulate writing teacher preferred anonymity. Like the brilliant writer/speaker Bourke Cockran (Winston Churchhill's

American mentor), she relegated herself to the shadows to make others great.

I met Phyllis Heald while hosting "The Writing World" television show (interviewing authors, poets, editors, agents, publishers...). Made aware of her accomplishments by several guests, and having heard the interesting "missing word" story about how she became an American, I anticipated an entertaining interview. She refused my invitation. Sometime later, when one of her celebrity clients said, "I shudder to think of where I'd be today if Phyllis Heald had not been born American," I tried again, unsuccessfully. Not until I sought her advice about my writing would I be privileged to know this remarkable woman--but I never got my interview.

Briefly, this is her story.

Her Shakespearean-actor grandfather left England to seek fame and fortune on the American stage, planning to send for his family when he became a Broadway star. But success evaded him. Funds running out, he wired that he was coming home. To save money the telegram contained as few words as possible: "Sail on Wednesday." Long anticipating the news that it was time to come, his wife managed to secure passage on short notice and sailed with their three children on Wednesday.

The man and his family passed somewhere in mid ocean.

For want of the word "I" four people were now in America, only one in England. How to solve this dilemma? Money was the deciding factor. It would cost much less to return one person to the U. S., than four to England.

Of this stage actor's American family, one son grew up to be a famous Hollywood director (the Steven Spielberg of the 20s). His only child, blonde, blue-eyed, precocious Phyllis, traveled the world with her parents, became an actress, and planned to marry a businessman. But fate intervened. Someone introduced her to Weldon Heald, grandson of the governor of Vermont. Weldon was a writer.

As Mrs. Weldon Heald, Phyllis soon gave up acting for writing. Her interest sparked, surfaced her special affinity for words; and with every-day tutoring by a professional her inherent talent flourished. Together the creative team wrote six plays (five were produced on Broadway), several books, hundreds of magazine articles, essays and short stories. Then they began teaching, conducting writing classes, workshops and seminars throughout the western states.

After the death of her husband Phyllis just lived for writing. She published thousands of articles, short stores and scripts, winning national and state awards. She spoke at seminars, served as president of The Society of Southwestern Authors, president and regional director of Pen Women, president of Women in Communication... But her great contribution to the literary world (in my opinion) was helping, inspiring, and storing up fledgling writers. Only by word of mouth, her reputation flourished.

"That articulate, entertaining writing teacher who tells it like it is and always with generous doses of encouragement."

A full time writer's advocate, Phyllis Heald also chaired weekly round tables for literary friends (whom she supported for decades), while critiquing manuscripts from all over the country, for nil.

Combining more than half a century of experience with special insight and expertise, this popular manuscript doctor never lacked for patients. Students and clients streamed to her door like vagrants to a free clinic. As one of them, I felt especially blessed. She became my mentor, and dear friend. By sterling example I found my niche, on the alternate road.

Several of today's top authors credit her for their success. One, who wishes to remain anonymous, said "What Ms. Heald taught me about writing was invaluable; but most importantly, she gave me the confidence I needed to aggressively promote my career."

This *good* writer, and self-promoter, now beams from the top of the ladder.

In the extraordinary career of his teacher however, self-promotion played no part. Phyllis Heald triumphed out of respect for the talent of all who live and work in the writing world. With altruism and dedication to the profession she worked to awake the sleeping genius in every would-be writer. No one believed more in the power of the written word.

"Words have the power to open the eyes of the world," she once told me. "Right words well presented, more than any other creative form, can stir emotions and give vent to thoughts and dreams that soar."

As a serious writer you want to help open the eyes of the world. If you feel you are missing the chance, if your career is not progressing, if the thoughts you marshal onto paper are not being published in big money markets, and the publicity route is offensive, perhaps the writing road less taken is for you.

Phyllis Heald's charitable gift to literature cannot be overemphasized. She made everybody she met a better writer. By her dedication they realized the joy of creating. And her contribution was never-ending. At 90 she was still taking telephone calls at 4:30 a.m., when her workday (and mine) began. As for her personal satisfaction, consider: a desk creaking under piled high manuscripts awaiting their turn, a mailbox overflowing with invitations, awards and gifts—and the invaluable appreciation of struggling writers who became lifelong friends.

Writing career **extraordinary**? What do you think?

NECESSITY

Without a mentor
the writer lives
laborious days,
a loner
locked in solitude,
suffering under
a cloud of doubt,
forever
riding the see-saw
up from possibility,
down to out.

In the literary
comedy of error,
the novice
pays heavily
(sometimes never
tops out over worry)
without a mentor.

THE INDISPENSIBLE TOOL

"The art of writing cannot be learned all at once."

This 18th century observation by Jean Jacques Rousseau, still rings true. No matter how great your natural talent or how long you have been writing don't think you are above mistakes. When carried away with enthusiasm for our subject it's easy to get careless about details and slip back into amateur habits. Every writer slips sometime.

Every writer needs a checklist.

This indispensable tool, which in the beginning you relied on, should not be discarded. After your teacher or mentor gave you the basics, you kept it at your elbow, and referred to it often. And, always, just before submitting you went down the list:

Is the title interesting?
Is the lead grabbing?
Strong, active verbs?
Used adjectives rarely?
Varied sentence structure?
Paragraph length varied?
Transitions smooth?
Details instead of generalities?

These are just a few examples. Your list will be different; you first list will be long. As you become more experienced, more confident you will cut it down to just the few that plague you. Then one day you might decide that you no longer need it.

Down the line you'll discover that you do. You may even want to add to it. Old habits start sneaking back; and experience teaches you new errors to watch for. Invest in a little insurance; take a few minutes to update your list. It's more than a bad day at the office for a writer who loses a sale, if she's also racked with guilt—for discovering an error too late. Don't leave yourself open to the possibility.

The key to progress in any endeavor is discovering, and remembering, your weak points. Reminders at your elbow will help hold you on the professional track. Just as you use an outline so you won't wander, use a checklist to insure against inherent tendencies that shout amateur. You know what they are; list them.

Maybe you habitually embroider with adjectives and adverbs, get overzealous and become flowery? How about redundancy? Forget to use metaphors and similes? Perhaps your pet words keep cropping up, or you overwork the verb to be. An editor friend once told me he spots a beginner by overuse of is, are, was, and were.

We all have reasons for a checklist. I struggle most with an inherent urge to qualify every statement; I use too many prepositional phrases, and overuse the coma--can't seem to cure myself of *"comaitis."* What do you keep forgetting?

According to a *Reader's Digest* editor, "What writers tend to forget most is the power of short, sharp sentences."

In the past long sentences, like long paragraphs of description, were in style. Readers felt robbed if not given full-blown word pictures of every scene and setting. In olden days people read more leisurely. We live a faster life. And since TV pictures the world for us bits and pieces are usually enough. Today trimmed to the bone articles, like slimmed to the bone models, make the big money. If you are guilty of padding, or dragging it out, make a note to jog your memory.

For whatever you have to watch, add a reminder. Your customized, updated, *advanced* list should include every new error you discover. Maybe just yesterday you learned about avoiding jargon, using plain instead of fancy words, putting the word you want to emphasize at the beginning or end of the sentence ... And of course check for the all time standard of good writing—clarity.

Nothing beats making sure that your message is clear and understandable to someone reading it cold.

How do you do that? By reading it cold yourself. After sweating over your creation for weeks, or months, put it aside for a week, a month, however long it takes to get the subject completely out of your mind. By working on something else, forget it (as much as you can); then if your imagination is elastic enough, try reading it as if someone else wrote it. This in order to experience the story as an acquisitions editor will.

When giving your work that final reading to determine if the message reads exactly as you intended, always keep in mind that "you can't get away with hot air in cold print."

Perhaps this quote should be typed across the top of every checklist. If you're speaking and something you say doesn't make sense to your listeners they'll probably just shrug and forget it. But when they're reading, you are wide open to censure. The reader has the time and opportunity to go back and double check what led up to a statement they didn't understand. And after re-reading prior sentences (maybe ambiguous) trying to pick up the thread of your thought, if they still can't decipher the sense of it, you can expect to lose a reader. What's more, by word-of-mouth you'll lose others.

During the long haul from novice to professional keep a constant look out for the stumbling blocks. Know from the start that stagnation, rejection, and disillusion all play a part in undermining the writer. Ups and downs are the norm. That's how it is. Also, should you have a surge of success, expect post-success pitfalls. Many a race to the top has turned into a long dry summer. If you hit a drought, before you rage at the editors look hard in the mirror. Is it possible you slipped? Or you suffer from a temporary rash of carelessness.

But if you keep an updated checklist the cure is readily at hand.

As you advance up the ladder in your specialty, that old "the one that gets used" tool will wear down like an everyday pencil; but it's never safe to dispose of it. Originally, long, strong, and indispensable it pulled you out of the chorus line of barely salable writing. Worn down and updated, it will get your star billing.

LINGUISTIC FAILINGS

By careless words,
human confounding ...

Like buildings
brick by brick crumble,
like relationships
hurt by hurt fail,
thoughts made readable
(like sounds invisible)
enter the air with
metaphysical power.

Born of innocent letters
strung together carelessly,
words can spawn a river
of angry – the receiver,
reacting instantly, as if blood
were deliberately sent,
failing to consider what
might have been meant...

And again the killing,
for lack of linguistic honor.

WRITERS' TREASURE HOUSE

Every working writer has access to a thesaurus, in book form or on line. I'm sure. What writer would be without one? Yet few fully utilize it. Do you? Do you realize what a treasure it is?

In Latin *thesaurus* means "treasure house."

In reality this writer's helper is much more than a word finder with synonyms and antonyms. It's a wealth of possibilities for the right choice. Within its pages you'll discover jewels that will dress up your writing with sparkle and magic, as well as the precise word to sting, soothe, arouse … maybe start a landslide of thought.

As writers are acutely aware, thoughts are things. And words are working witnesses, conveyors of our thoughts to readers. We can't afford to haphazardly select them. Thankfully, we have a thesaurus. Each time I need a special word capable of striking a blow, or kindling a flame, when a new interesting word pregnant with a particular meaning is imperative, I feel greatly indebted to the 19th century student of philosophy who conceived it.

The original "book of names for same or similar objects" resulted from the false imprisonment of a young Swiss intellectual named Peter Mark Roget. As a hobby Roget made lists of words that were related. And to sharpen his perception of ideas attempted to divide thought into categories. During his year in prison, the hobby becoming full time, he succeeded in preparing a repertory of myriad different groups of related words. And when released he continued adding to his collection. Finally in 1852 *A Thesaurus of English Words and Phrases* was published.

That first edition, meant for philosophers, immediately became popular among writers, emerging as an essential tool. Soon the word thesaurus became synonymous with word finder, the name Roget with all future editions. Subsequent additions, beginning with one by his son, multiplied into dozens of versions, revisions, and improvisations. All "to help you find the word you want, or have been unable to think of."

This turned out to be an understatement (like clothes cover the body). Clothes also keep you warm, advertise your vocation, make fashion assertions, and camouflage figure imperfections, among other things. A thesaurus supplies new words, forgotten words, and better words, as well as the magic word that is just right. This ever-ready word-suggester can raise your writing from ho hum to interesting. Use it every day to improve clarity and impress your reader-- especially that most important first reader, an acquisitions editor. If ever you think editors don't understand your intent, consider the possibility that you didn't make it clear. Often it is for lack of better wording that we miss an opportunity.

Upon re-reading a rejected manuscript, if you are not given a reason, try to think about what you wrote from another perspective. To someone of a different background the words you used might have a different connotation. Whether you are in the business of informing, or entertaining, study your words, know them, check for every shade of meaning. With the help of a good thesaurus write clearer composition. Leave no editor in doubt of what you are trying to say, and you will have more readers.

Of course all brains don't work alike. Someone might misconstrue a well-written meaning. But most times, we must admit, being misunderstood is our own fault. Word choice cannot be overemphasized. It's the writer's responsibility to track down the best, most *exact* word to convey the intended meaning. Take the time in every instance to consult your thesaurus. It's invaluable, maybe more essential than a dictionary. If you learn to utilize it and never settle for the *almost* right word, your writing will soon warrant money. Certainly, the author of this famous quote was well paid.

"The difference between the right word and the almost right word, is like the difference between lightning and the lightning bug."

We always laugh at that quip by Mark Twain (and we're supposed to; humor was his forte). But do we fully appreciate the wisdom of it? Mark Twain wrote unsurpassed American prose. By concentrating on finding the right word every time he made his sentences sing, and left no guesswork for the editor, or the reader. Therefore, his simple stories gripped and held our interest--and became classics.

After you make your best selections and complete your stories or articles, after they've cooled, give them one last test. Make sure that each and every word fits. If the noun is good, and picturesque, if the verb is strong and active, you may have satisfied the basics of good writing.

But the manuscript isn't ready for submission until you have determined that each selected word *works,* for just what you want to convey— and no other could replace it.

Writers always want to know the reason a manuscript is rejected. And I'm sorry to tell you that we are not often given the reason. Sometimes that's because editors don't want to tell you; sometimes they just don't bother; other times they don't know. If an editor can't identify a reason, most probably it's a case of misinterpretation.

And after your book is published, if it receives mixed reviews, are the reviewers mixed up? Or is it that each reviewer understands your wording differently? Different interpretations depend on background, education, and personality, all of which are beyond your control. That's why writing teachers emphasize using short words, and tell you to "*always* select the word in common usage."

Misunderstanding through misinterpretation, has long been a universal problem. People seeking peace must first understand each other, as writers seeking to be published must first be understood.

Insure your writing will be correctly interpreted. Take the time to "dig" for the special gem cut to your exact specification. Find the one that will paint the right picture. And when there is one that will replace two or three, use it; look until you find it. It behooves every writer to develop the thesaurus habit.

Word choice. Word magic. The right word every time. Thesaurus fidelity will boost your rate of acceptance. Guaranteed.

GOLDEN KEY

Poetry is
a shining elixir,
a golden key.

Translating
baseness
into beauty,
calming disorder,
revealing the inner
(unmasking),
it shows us
sameness in
diversity,
helps us see
the soul of
another.

Poetry
opens the
invisible door.

THE POWER OF POETRY

Poetic writing that proclaims and promotes truth has been called "the most immortal thing on this mortal earth." Yet, by the twentieth century it had almost faded from existence.

From the beginning of writing for thousands of years the poets sat beside the rulers. Revered and favored, their influence over conscious thought was notable. They wrote history, philosophy, and entertained (the first novels were written in poetry). Deemed the architects of doctrine, and translators of vision, poets once influenced every aspect of people's lives.

Then the industrial age roared in with its fast-paced progress, speedy transportation, radio, television, electronic technology ... Emerged the push-button age, and the "antiquated art" dropped into oblivion. Only an old stogy would read poetry. The masses watched TV--wisdom and diversion served up in action, light, sound and color, all at the touch of a button.

The poet-star had fallen.

But, after decades of ostracism the intrinsic human hunger for the art that touches heart, mind, and senses resurfaced. About mid-way into the 20th century, as people began admitting to deeper thought, poetry began rising from the ashes. And with the universal language returning to majority favor, gradually, those who wrote it were no longer stigmatized. The modern poet does not receive top billing (and may never again), but is again accepted by society.

What sparked the turn-about?

A professor friend of mine credits President Kennedy. "Look back," he said, "and you'll see that the resurgence of public interest in poetry commenced right after JFK asked Robert Frost to compose and read a poem for his inauguration."

Also Kennedy personally promoted the art. These words from one of his speeches were often quoted in the sixties.

"When power leads men towards arrogance, poetry reminds him of his limitations. When power narrows the area of man's concern, poetry reminds him of the richness and diversity of his own existence. When power corrupts, poetry cleanses."

Many people believe that poetry possesses power. Universally, immortal power has been attributed to the art "which most effectively commands the imagination and most deeply expresses the spirit." According to Native American poet Linda Hogan, poetry is "a large spiritual undertaking." Siberian poet Yevgeny Yevtushenko refers to Russian poetry as "the spiritual newspaper." Throughout the world as people cease ignoring their spirituality, poetry rises.

In 1995 several psychics predicted "spirituality growing and spreading among all the different peoples of the planet." A local pastor called that good news for humanity. He believes, "the recent public interest in poetry reveals an inherent human need for the *internal* experience missing in a technological society."

Today's poets are happy to fill that need, which runs the gamut from surrealism to raw-living immediacy. They not only tackle the usual subjects (life, love, and death), but sexism, racism, politics, murder, drugs ... all the ills of our society. And while modern poets create their varied versions of the recognized power for healing--and bringing people together, television projects it to the world. Example: Bill Moyers' programs on PBS stations.

When introducing the first program of the series, "The Power of the Word," Moyers said, "Poets have power, the power of the word, to create a world of thought and emotion others can share."

The popular TV series, featuring William Stafford, Gerald Stern, Sharon Olds, Robert Bly and others, addressed powerful subjects like "Voices of Memory" and "Where the Soul Lives." Later programs also included poetry therapy in "Healing and the Mind." These shows (and their imitators) received wide acclaim, resulting in mass video sales--making video and audio poetry big business, which revived readings. Poetry on radio keeps proliferating. And the publishing world is succumbing to "the art of the heart."

Now many slick magazines include a poetry page (or pages); in the past we were lucky if they published one or two poems for fillers. Literary publications keep devoting more and more space to poetry. Some now print every kind and form by poets at every level. We find light verse, epigrams, and haiku in house organs, company newsletters, and church bulletins. Newspapers print political and opinion poetry, as does the local daily, in addition to the usual humorous and seasonal.

Today, some version of "the language of life" is available to every segment of society. Poetry is everywhere, even in hotel rooms.

The American Poetry and Literary Project (co-founded by Columbia University graduate Andrew Carroll and Nobel Prize winning poet Joseph Brodsky) donates books of poetry to hotel chains across the country. "Because poetry is the perfect balm for a weary traveler." Brodsky and Carroll believe strongly in their project. Their goal is to "place an anthology of poetry in every hotel and motel room in the nation."

As a result of this renaissance (the return of poetry to the masses) poetic writing now makes money--for some. The dollar sign entered the picture with the advent of poetry slams in shopping malls and "cowboy poets" being interviewed on the Johnny Carson show. The hucksters awakened to the surprising fact that poetry influenced the great majority of their buyers. USA Today reported the result of a survey which documented steady increases in the use of poetry in advertising, most notably in television commercials.

It can be argued, of course, that commercial poetry is far from literary. But "the elite language" in any form, again being accepted, used, and serving the public is remedial. That the weary world is no longer deaf to the voice of the muse, means progress in human relations.

In the past, when the power of poetry was universally recognized, bards like Milton (who sacrificed his eyes for cultural progress) served the people of his time without ceasing. By braving the miseries of the world and exposing the mysteries of heaven, John Milton dutifully earned the title, "The splendid bridge from the Old World to the new."

Now, the new and the old worlds joined by electronic technology, maybe the working poets of the planet can fill in the chasm. Science and poetry collaborating might one day close the gaps between fighting segments of society. As evidenced by a swelling membership in The International Society of Poets for Peace, modern bards from many countries are working toward that end. In the "divine mission" of universal understanding could poetry possibly succeed where everything else has failed?

Some believe the art with the power that illuminates underlying sameness in differences, awakens souls, opens hearts ... can lead us out of ourselves and make us grow as human beings.

In an interview while serving as National Poet Laureate, Rita Dove credited poetry for her personal growth. Finding life in her youth to be raw and confusing, she discovered that "Only poetry possessed the tentacles to reach the truth of it." And now a master of the power, this popular poet helps others reach the truth in their lives. It's believable that her profound writings make a contribution.

But poetry need not be profound to help human kind. There's power also in light verse. Humorous poetry projects joy and fantasy. The rhythm and beauty of lyrical poetry can be soothing, uplifting, sometimes revealing. Licensed to write free, peeling to the essence, the poet makes a difference. Every poem ever written (when it hits home and is understood) will help someone. And the one who writes it always benefits.

William Butler Yeates once said, "The pleasure of poetry is one tenth recognition, nine tenths satisfaction."

If you're a poet, or aspire to be, enjoy the creative high, the fulfillment, the legacy of poetry to one who writes it. And should you be a poetic genius blessed with *the power*, enjoy the honor—however and whenever it comes.

One who believed in the immortal power of poetry told this story.

A new arrival in heaven, witnessing a parade of the world's greatest poets, recognized Homer and Dante near the front, but not the little man ahead of them. In the eyes of God an unknown was the greatest poet. (related by Mark Twain).

PRICELESS PICTURES

Poetry
is reality
best dressed,
sincerity,
love expressed
in beauty --
priceless pictures
of a century --
and rare times,
in purity,
a glimpse
of eternity.

SEE MORE OF YOUR POETRY IN PRINT

If you are serious about your poetry you may constantly think about seeing it in print. Don't.

When a poem first comes to you don't muddy the inspirational flow with mundane thoughts of label, of what an editor might think, of what is salable ... Allow the idea free reign to develop naturally, purely. And after you put the raw concept into form on paper concentrate on polishing and perfecting it. Then, think about publishing it. Then come down off your literary high, to business—or your gem may lay undiscovered for years.

Emily Dickinson wrote 1700 poems. Only seven of them were published while she lived. Think about that. Her great talent unrecognized, her profound messages unread, until long after her death--because she would not leave her ivory tower to venture into the business of selling. By all accounts her art was everything. A lover of solitude, inherently adverse to commercialism, and publicity shy, she lived only for *writing* poetry. Marketing it was left to her heirs.

In the arts, as in any business, the best rises to recognition by astute marketing. Nothing sells itself. And according to Robert Frost, "poets have to be more business-like than business men."

The garret poet may block out reality; but let us face it. If we want people to read our poetry we must master the determinants of acceptance and ferret out the publishers that will print it. At first, this seems an overwhelming challenge. I find beginning poets baffled by the marketing maze. So many questions, so little they know about publishing. And after years of dreaming, overly anxious, suffering under a cloud of doubt that it will ever happen.

If you're worrying that you may not see your poetry in print, take heart; you will—if you follow these primary pointers to publication.

Send your first efforts to beginner's magazines (to editors who advertise that they accept from beginners). By submitting to magazines that are wide open to new talent you give yourself the best possible chance. Usually these are small publications, paying in copies, or nil, or nothing. Sometimes they are poorly edited; but that editor may still know more than you do, and having solicited your work will almost always help you. Why? Because having just launched the magazine she is desperate to get enough material for the first few issues. But that editor also wants her publication to make a good showing; she isn't going to print everything as it comes in. So expect to allow her "liberties" as a condition for acceptance.

As long as you are not asked to compromise your principles, don't be adamantly against suggested changes. Take advice you wouldn't ordinarily, if it seems conditional on being published. Hide your pride and admit you're a novice. Do *almost* anything it takes to be published the first few times; for nothing, absolutely nothing, boosts a beginner's confidence like seeing his creation in print. And confidence is a habit forming "upper." Success builds on success.

Every famous writer, from Hawthorne to Steinbeck to "the poet of paradise," first published in some obscure quarterly. Surely, some helpful editors offered them advice and assistance, which may or may not have been necessary. On the other hand, sometimes what a generous editor tells you can almost add up to a free writing course. Certainly, submitting several times to an encouraging editor accelerates the learning-by-doing process. In all probability if you follow instructions and show appreciation (and were good at all to start with) you'll have your first acceptance. If not, nothing lost, and valuable knowledge gained. As a bonus you may have made an editor friend.

Of course you can expect that new, *hungry* publication to be more particular later. But if you've made a friend there, at least your work will be familiar when they have a steady stream of submissions to choose from. And because of the experience, you have become a better writer. You are now in the running, comparable to some of your competition.

Repeat this performance a few times, then search out some of the better known literary magazines willing to consider poetry from a *promising* beginner. Plan to work up gradually to paying markets, learning some of the quirks of the trade as you go. After you've been submitting for a while you will discover that "overstocked" is the number one reason given for rejection. And it may not always be true. It's just easier for a busy editor (requiring no further explanation). You will also discover that many new editors/publishers are aspiring poets like you, who didn't see their dream coming true, but were lucky to have money... After a discouraging bout of rejection, they decided to establish a market of assured acceptance.

For those who have the confidence, patience, and fortitude this is an alternate route to recognition. I know a good poet who tried it and is now happier in his role as editor. He enjoys being in a position to help others, and besides seeing his poetry in print, has made a success of his magazine (you might recognize the name of it).

If you're not interested in such a venture, but only in getting your poetry published, search out new editors. Looking back down the road, they are naturally disposed to help other strugglers.

Consult "current" market listings. Information in the latest *Poet's Market* may be a year old. It's often more than a year after statistics are received by the publisher until the book is organized, edited, published, and out. During that time editors come and go, policies change, magazines fold, they are bought and sold... Easily up to twenty percent of the listings in the latest *Poet's Market* could be yesterday's data. Look in periodicals for updated, and late, market information.

Note that many emerging poetry journals and literary magazines trade ads with like publications—and publish each other's poetry. When you repeatedly see the same half dozen names under poems in those same publications, realize that it means little opportunity for outsiders.

Make it a habit to check local newspapers, pamphlets, company magazines, house organs, religious publications--every piece of printed matter in sight. You'll be surprised how many now contain poetry. Today, poetry is "in." There are marketing possibilities everywhere and every week new ones. Once in a health store I discovered a diet magazine with a "poetry page." On impulse I went home, quickly selected three poems that might fit, and sent them in.

What a change, and a surprise. Immediate acceptance of all three, plus *money*! The pay was twenty dollars for six lines. And I saw the first poem in print just a month later. However, there was a downer side. They never published or paid for the other two. The magazine folded after three issues.

Determine your competition. Seriously study your target. How many pages in the magazine? Do they print only poetry, or is that space shared with prose? How may poems per issue? And is it monthly, quarterly or annually? Analyze your chances by how many poems they publish per issue, compared to the number of submissions they say they receive. Check the percentages. Do they buy 70 percent of the poems they receive? 30 percent? Or ten? If ten or below, acceptance from a beginner would be like winning the lottery. Be kind to yourself. Don't hang your hopes on impossible odds.

Send for sample copies (as many as you can afford). For all too often what you read in the guidelines and what you see printed are two different things. If the market listing said "accepts all kinds," but eighteen out of twenty are free verse, don't chance a traditional. If "no taboos subject-wise," but you don't find a political or religious, don't send one. What about the length of the poems? All under thirty lines, as the guidelines say? There, too, go by what you see. Or shorter.

An editor friend told me, "If I haven't seen their work before, and I am hesitant, I might squeeze in an eight-liner, but not something longer."

Be meticulous about manuscript mechanics. Remember the power of first impression. Give your poetry the best chance with an impressable presentation: clean copy, neatness, the right format, regular font styles, in standard size, correct grammar, and no misspellings.

The birth of your poem is between you and the muse, or your inner voice; but its introduction to the world is between you and a selected editor. Don't turn him off with a careless offering. Check, check, and double check. Be sure your spelling is for the intended word, and the word correctly conveys your meaning. For one word used incorrectly an editor gave me a half page grammar lesson, and sent all my poems back.

Allow the law of averages to work for you. The late Judson Jerome (*Poet's Market* and the *Writer's Digest* poetry column) was quoted as keeping "thirty poems in the mail all the time." My count averages forty. With thousands of poets submitting to the same publications you're not in the game with a paltry few. Send each editor the maxim number of poems allowed (no more). She can't respond to those not in her waiting pile. And we never know which one of the few, carefully selected to fit that publication, might appeal to, or match the mood of, that editor that day.

As in any game of chance you won't beat all the odds; you can't even know them. But take a big leap in faith instead of a little one. Consider every minute mention in the guidelines. Take time to send a first class package. With all the time you've invested in creating your poetry you can't afford to submit it haphazardly.

And one tip about economy. To pay less for postage you might try using thinner than twenty pound paper (but not flimsy or erasable). Two rate hikes ago I went to fifteen pound for poetry, to send one more poem for one stamp, and so far no editor has objected.

Study the editor. After you've been playing this pitch and hope game for a few years it will strike you that character, personality, and idiosyncrasy all take part in the play. I once submitted the same four poems to two editors (simultaneous submissions accepted). From research and guidelines study both seemed to be equally promising markets for philosophical poetry. But …

One promptly responded with laudatory praise. " … happy to accept them all. We so seldom get any good thoughtful poems." The other sent a form letter rejection with two curt words written on the bottom. "Don't preach," underlined in red.

Two people can publish the same kind of magazine, and print the same type of poetry, but think quite differently.

If subject matter is not spelled out in guidelines, do a little sleuthing. The name of the publication is often a key to what they will print. You might have to look up the word in the dictionary; but the meaning can be quite revealing as to the character and interests of the editor/publisher.

Go through your sample copy with the proverbial fine toothed comb. Does the subject matter of the printed poems vary widely? Or do they mostly seem to adhere to the same line of thought? Your poem must say something that editor likes to hear. Should it also conform to a preferred style, free verse, traditional, narrative, lyric? Or are they all mixed in? And what about length, are the majority of the poems short, one page, several pages?

In trying to discover what editors will publish look for their work, in other magazines as well as their own. Study their poems, the poems they've published, and their guidelines to the letter. And when you receive a response if you're lucky to find a handwritten note scribbled on the printed form, take time to decipher it. A busy editor rarely writes on a printed form.

The hard reality … good poetry, like beauty, is in the eye of the beholder. Editors accept what they like. One even had it printed across the bottom of his guidelines. "If you place poetry with us it's probably because you think like we do."

How to see more of your poetry in print? Ferret out all the facts—and the editors who think like you do.

BY POETRY . . .

By the paradox freedoms and further reaches
of poetry I break my mountains loose;
they smother the valley, muting the noises
of yesterday; and through the dust I see
the family--the connection, the interaction
between humanity and nature.

Escaping the pressure, engaging the inner,
with poetry, I draw maps of consciousness,
pull fractured memory to surface, and find
the parallels. Then working the questions,
by-passing the burdens of history, I knit it
all together: still life, plant life, animal life,
human—the whole living spectrum.

By reach of poetry we open, as by death.
We play no part in dying; heaven sets us free
from controlling time. But at our setting sun
we who are endowed with mind awaken to the
fracture—finally honor the human, animal,
nature family—by poetry, or by death.

WRITERS HELPING EACH OTHER

Writers, poets, painters, musicians (all who pursue a career in the arts) desperately need the support of their peers. Not only in perfecting their art, but also in their struggle against the inevitable—the misunderstanding (and often resentment) of the traditional working world.

Nine-to-fivers, and those who don't recognize labor in nonphysical occupations, label us lightweights. The consensus: writers only work when they want to … play in the middle of the day … take a vacation whenever…

And when we make money we're "lucky stiffs." In general, writers are stereotyped self-isolated dreamers defying convention and neglecting friends and family, although most of us don't fit the stereotype. But sometimes we are guilty in part. And then there are the "sluffers. " Those who play at writing to avoid working give the dream killers justification for their actions.

Society is not entirely judgmental, but people who nag, ("get a real job"), the controllers who try to block your every attempt at creativity, those who demand all your time, and those who belittle your talent are more than enough to deal with. How many of you have friends who try to joke you out of being so serious about what they call your "hobby?" Unless you're lucky, expect to have one or more of these situations to combat. Plus the waiting for praise from family. Sometimes that's like standing on a hill top waiting for a floating feather to reach the bottom of the canyon. There are families who unite in deliberate attempts to prevent the pursuit of a literary career.

Of course there are supportive families too. But generally serious writers are forever challenged for their deviance from the norm, and doomed to do constant battle for the chance to practice their art.

A.R.T.S. Anonymous to the rescue.

Are you familiar with the national support group for "coping in the arts?" Since 1984 this organization of noncompetitive mutual support has been helping writers win their personal battles. Modeled after Alcoholics Anonymous, its 72 chapters nationwide provide encouragement and full time assistance to anyone learning to live the lifestyle conducive to their particular creativity. A.R.T.S. will help with a financial situation, a mental block, procrastination, loneliness … Whatever your problem, you will not be judged. Even if it has to do with your own nonproductive attitude or habits. The procedure is to pair the one who seeks help with a peer of more experience, "who listens with interest and dispenses friendly advice."

Sounds too good to be true? Check them out. For complete information about their 12-point program contact A.R.T.S. Anonymous, P. O. Box 320175, New York, NY 10023, or A.R.T.S.Anonymous.com. Morale building publications, and literature recovery material are available in a number of inexpensive pamphlets.

Mutual one on one spirit boosting may also be found in the local writing club that the loner hesitates to join. If you are feeling especially alone why not reconsider? The experience of socializing with fellow writers will uplift you, as will the benefits of networking. Very possibly at the first meeting someone will answer your plaguing question. More importantly, contacting people who talk your language and understand your frustrations will reap a greater benefit. Writer friends.

National writers' organizations provide a wider variety of support; but unless you live in the same city personal contact is lacking. Your questions (by telephone, e-mail, or correspondence) may wait a long time for an answer. The information, however, will be worth waiting for.

Following are three far-reaching associations worth contacting. All have maintained a reputation for exceptional assistance to writers.

THE NATIONAL WRITERS ASSOCIATION (NWA). This sixty-year-old club stands ready to assist its members "in every aspect of the writing life." Anyone interested in any branch of writing may join. Services run from basic assistance on a first manuscript to selling a book, including critiques, contract review, agent referral and complaint settlement. NWA also publishes a bimonthly magazine (*Authorship*), a comprehensive monthly newsletter, market updates, a home study course, and research reports "on every subject remotely related to writing." In addition, they periodically issue *The Professional Freelance Writer's Directory*. Contact Sandra Whelchel, Executive Director, National Writers Association, 3140 South Peoria, #295, Aurora, CO 80014.

POETS AND WRITERS, INC. This nationwide network of literary experts (not a club—no membership fee) publishes *Poets and Writers Magazine,* a thick quarterly of indispensable information to help writers help themselves. It has been called "The Wall Street Journal of the Writing Profession." Other publications (written by top writers and editors of *Poets and Writers Magazine)* include *The Writing Business,* a popular handbook updated periodically, and an annual *Directory of American Poets and Fiction Writers* (check to see if you qualify for a listing). They also staff The Poets and Writers Information Center, open access Monday through Friday 11 a.m. to 3 p.m. eastern standard time, telephone (212) 226-3586. Or contact Poets and Writers, 72 Spring Street, NY 10012. Website: www.pw.org.

THE SOCIETY OF SOUTHWESTERN AUTHORS (SSA), a nonprofit organization of writers and publishing professionals with a three level membership (associate, professional, and honorary). This most helpful organization, boasting members from all over the country, and Mexico, has been a mainstay in assisting aspiring writers and improving relationships with editors and publishers since 1972. Their seminars feature workshop leaders and participants from all over the U. S. and several foreign countries; the key speakers are household names. The annual conferences offer dual level instruction in nonfiction, poetry, fiction of every genre, public relations, and scripts. Monthly meetings, member contests, and *The Write Word* newsletter, provide members with valuable writing tips, contact information and peer recognition. SSA also publishes an annually updated membership roster.

To help promote the careers of their members SSA arranges media attention at well-publicized award banquets, public readings, and book signing parties. They also sponsor writing contests, student scholarships and student-writer chapters at accredited colleges. Contact President, SSA, or memberships chairman, at Box 30355, Tucson, Arizona 85751.

If you specialize, one of these organizations might prove helpful.

Western Writers of America, % Rita Cleary, WWA Membership, 20 Cove Woods Road, Oyster Bay, NY 11771; Mystery Writers of America, Inc., 17 East 47th Street, 6th Floor, New York, NY 10017, Romance Writers of America, 3707 FM 1960 West, Suite 55, Houston, TX 77068, Society of Children's Book Writers, SCBWI 8271 Beverly Blvd. Los Angeles, CA 90048.

For poets, the larger, better known supporters are The Academy of American Poets, www.poets.org, and The Poetry Society of America, www.poetrysociety.org.

You can also join The National Writers Union, which intercedes on members' behalf, most often assisting with contracts and grievances (they don't give legal advice). Website: www.nwu.org.

If you're adamantly a non-joiner, and don't have a teacher or mentor, there are alternate sources of information and advice quite readily available. Help is out there. Sometimes it's forthcoming from professional writers of reputation (they remember their days of struggle). Several who have it made are known to share their hard earned knowledge, when courteously asked.

For the price of a telephone call or letter (with SASE) beginners have been known to receive a wealth of insight and coveted support. According to John Irving, "Few writers, young or old, are really seeking advice; they want support." They usually get it.

In the writing world, I'm happy to say, the dirty game of stepping on heads to climb higher is not often played. Win any way you can tactics are unnecessary. For no one writes exactly like you do; no two writers maintain an equal level of expertise. Nor is an achievement point attained in any way lessened by aiding another's climb. Each goal we set and reach is not a plateau, only another high point.

At the highest point of his career, author/playwright, Maurice Masterlink modestly claimed, "it's just another starting point for better endeavor." He had long before determined, as most career writers do, that "*arrival* would mean no more exciting journeyings." Cervantes, too, thought the road was "always better than the inn." Most seasoned writers agree that helping fellow travelers heightens the adventure.

Saul Bellow, however, has been quoted as saying, "Writers seldom wish other writers well." I doubt that he meant it; I hope he didn't. I've found writers at all levels helping each other. And like good teachers, they not only show interest but also follow up, becoming mentors. It's a natural progression when you love the business you're in.

It is my wish that each of you on your path to success (with help from many sources) will feel inclined to help others reach their writing goal. Be an "uplifter," a cheerleader, a Good Samaritan on another writer's road. Every chance you get, share your knowledge, or tell someone "you can do it." And if you need a confidence boost, don't hesitate to reach out to your peers.

When we nourish another writer's dream, empowering someone to be more creative, humanity benefits. By free exchange of expertise and sharing of knowledge, the circle widens …

A world of writers helping each other.

DESTINED

Every talent
individuality,
that holy spark
of inner fire
encased in
an identity
of clay,
is pre-assigned
a different note
--and destined
to play
in harmony.

NEW YEAR THOUGHTS

Every New Year after the bells ring out excitement, anticipation, and hope, after the celebrating, writers return to their solitude and deliberate the customary resolution—to be a better writer.

But *how* do we think about it?

Unless we've just made a big sale we reminisce regrets and resolve never to do this or that again. Faced with a blank calendar, jogged by the media, conscience, tradition, before we make one mark on the new blank sheet we trot out the old errors, and berate ourselves for every minuscule failure. This all too common practice is a procrastination ruse, and leads to depression.

Don't get in the habit.

Rehashing the past before facing the future is beneficial. We learn from it. But give the practice as little time as possible. By mulling over rejections and other knockdowns you are accentuating the negative, which saps your strength. After a cursory review of what last year's errors taught you, blot out all thoughts of error. You're *one-up* when you face the fresh page with an untroubled mind.

Each new year arrives unmarked; but written all over it in invisible ink are possibilities and second chances that no past year has offered. This is opportunity unlimited. This year's bells could be a musical introduction to a fabulous career, if you don't start on a negative note.

Writer's New Year's Resolutions, published by The Writer's Digest School, doesn't even suggest reviewing failures; and all their resolutions are positive statements. "I resolve to daily study … to find new and fresh ideas … to write and re-write … to submit on a continual and regular schedule…" The list ends with the popular affirmation. "I shall be a better writer at the end of this year."

Almost every one of us will resolve to be a better writer. But working toward that accomplishment, busy meeting deadlines, sometimes we forget what we have determined needs improving. If you make resolutions do you remember what they were, and follow through?

At the beginning of every year, or any new cycle, we might also grade ourselves on the writer's code of ethics.

The National Writers Association "Code of Ethics and Standards of Practice," (furnished to all members) compels writers in every genre to recognize that constitutional guarantees of freedom of expression and freedom of the press imply responsibility, accuracy, verification of fact, and observance of the "fair use doctrine." In short, practicing writers are required to uphold the ideals of "justice, freedom, democracy and humanity."

Those who choose this dream vocation, by entertaining, educating, and building bridges to better understanding, have far reaching influence. As a writer you have the power to improve relationships between the races, the sexes, and the species. You can be helpful in mediating between neighbors, and countries. Or you can use that power for undermining, as some writers have been known to do. Whatever you create in any genre on any subject, when published, will produce thoughts and influence actions. Always keep this in mind. As a published writer you may have more influence, than you now imagine.

During my business career I once had a secretary who worshipped the written word. Anything she read in a book was gospel; anything published was fact. To her, spoken words might be contested, but never words in print. It seemed she couldn't conceive of a published error.

When you realize how easily some people can be influenced by what you write (and maybe differently from what you intended) responsibility weighs heavy. Remembering this woman, and the many others who swallow everything they read, frightens me into double and triple checking my work.

Knowing that the candle of truth burns faintly, and that even validated information is sometimes a smoke screen, writers should be ever wary. It's easy to compound the error of one gone before, unknowingly. And those labeled "authority" have sometimes been wrong. No matter, we must shoulder the responsibility to be as honest and accurate as humanly possible.

At the annual traditional time for renewal, when we rate ourselves, and resolve to eliminate the chaff that jades us, let us, also *will to follow through*. For without a doubt, that's what winners do.

I've witnessed several seemingly impossible successes from following through, or just hanging in there long enough.

One New Year's Day is indelibly stamped on my memory. Visiting a student who had been diagnosed with inoperable cancer, not expecting her to last the year, I pointedly avoided the subject of New Year's resolutions. But she would not be restrained from telling me hers. Under a cloud of pain and derogatory circumstance, ignoring everything against her, this aspiring writer of average ability announced, "I have resolved to publish something before I die."

And she did!

Whether you are beginning a writing career, or nursing a sick one, let your primary resolution be to clear your mind of negatives, and clutter. Allow no circumstance or mental inhibitions from the past to take part in your present. At the beginning of a new year let bygones yawn behind you, and all past errors die with December. Forget what might have been, and follow the example of nature. Spring spends no time worrying about the skeletal frame of winter, but gets busy growing again.

That's what we all should do after a cold downer.

From *The Writer's Prayer,* copyright 1972: "Lord, give me insight and sensitivity to people and events around me. Give me the ability to write wisely and well, to write in a way that will enrich and enlighten the hearts and minds of others. Give me the courage to write clean and true … and to have faith in myself and my talent, when no one else has faith in either."

Ever since New Year's resolutions became custom the wise and the famous have been advising faith in ourselves as the best remedy for improving our lives and economic situations. Still it tops most lists of suggested resolutions. These are also common. "Stop and smell the roses … smile more … keep your promises … forgive an injustice … drink more water … get up earlier … work harder…" and the oft' repeated words of wise old Ben Franklin. "Be at war with your vices, at peace with your neighbors, and let every new year find you a better man."

Today, Ben would have to say man *or woman*. But since colonial times there's been no change in the wisdom of his quote.

We all know that looking back does not expand one's horizon. In any career, and especially in writing, the prelude to success is a long struggle left behind. Whether novelist, poet, or member of "The Fourth Estate," we all reach maximum effectiveness by working hard, living right, and looking *forward*, with confidence.

Every time the bells ring out may I remember.
* May every New Year find me a better writer.

THOUGHT POWER

A thought is
a seed of immortality,
an invisible signal of
energy.
Unleashed by the mind
it takes wing,
and with the speed of
lightning,
joins the vocal army
to sing
a song to the world
--good or evil.

THE FOUR LETTER WORD FOR FAILURE

Perusing an old Reader's Digest Anthology, *Getting the Most Out of Life,* I noted the frequency with which one four-letter word was tagged killer of confidence, reason for failure, the common factor most detrimental to success and happiness. Three chapters addressed it exclusively.

In myriad books and articles I continually find references to its negative power over our lives. There are almost as many quotes about it as for love. One dictionary used two hundred words to describe it. Everywhere, advice on how to face it, down it, overcome it ...

What is this gripping malaise that like no other blocks progress, inhibits fulfillment, and kills careers (most notably, writing careers)?

It's FEAR.

Fear of criticism, fear of ridicule, fear of rejection. Constantly fighting the saboteur, writers cry for help to squelch it. Enticed by titles like "Do The Thing You Fear," How I Found Freedom From Fear," "The Conquest of Fear," they run down every suggested remedy, convinced that these authors are authorities. Whatever their early symptoms, surely professionals no longer suffer them.

Not true. Although recognized accomplishment is the best medicine, most eminent writers claim they were never cured.

In *The Conquest of Happiness* Bertrand Russell confirmed that no amount of recognition entirely eliminates the ailment. Plenty of money doesn't cure it either. In *Think and Grow Rich,* Napoleon Hill asks, "How many of the six ghosts of fear are standing in your way?" FDR's famous after Pearl Harbor quote, "The only thing we have to fear is fear itself," revealed a president's concern that the immobilizing, highly contagious condition called fear could cripple a nation's ability to protect itself.

Of course, everybody who heard the quote could relate to fear, so the statement was forever repeated; and he who uttered it got credit for wisdom. But the credit may be bogus; the thought was not original. I think the president, or his speechwriters, coined the sentence by paraphrasing two well-known authors.

"The thing of which I have most fear is fear."
-- Montaigne
"Nothing is so much to be feared as fear."
-- Thoreau

Throughout history fear has inhibited creativity. No writer ever escaped insecurity, worry, and doubt. Even Shakespeare said, "Our traitor doubts make us lose the good we oft might win, by fearing to attempt."

New writers feel especially vulnerable facing the unknown pitfalls of publishing, and what they don't know about selling. In *How to Get Happily Published*, Judith Appelbuam assigns a whole section to "Fighting the Fear of Hustling," a battle which every published writer must win if he wants to make money. This ignorance that isn't bliss, darkens our every tomorrow—until we think it through.

At worst, what can happen that is so terrible?

Ms. Applebaum is a publishing authority, and she insists that "Any mistakes you make will probably be both correctable and instructive. They will certainly not be fatal." Believe this. Fearful unbelief in your ability not only causes inaction, but deters the development of your talent. After a reasonable stretch of study and practice it's time to trust your inner knowing, and forge ahead. So you strike out a time or two, the experience is better than stagnant wishing. Those you emulate struck out too, maybe many times before they dared to ignore the fear they never conquered.

The worst that can happen is never daring.

Example. Because of fear and timidity this writer vegetates her life away. Ever dreaming instead of doing, she periodically signs on for another writing course, and another (not quite ready to play the game), then gives up again, and again. This woman, frozen into inaction by fear of criticism, after twenty years of not trying, is a basket case of literary anxieties, unfulfilled and unhappy.

Ralph Keys, a long time writing teacher, warns students and readers that this can happen. In his book, *The Courage to Write: How Writers Transcend Fear*, he talks about it at great length, and emphasizes, "Not writing at all constitutes the ultimate triumph of fear."

Every beginner fighting butterflies needs to know that those who make it to the pinnacle haven't necessarily triumphed over fear. They simply refuse to let fear win. In his last interview the late Robert Davies, Canada's most lauded man of letters, let his admirers, and the world, in on his struggle. He said, "I'm foolishly open to destructive criticism ... my digestion, sleep, and far the worst, my self confidence is shattered..."

Whether you're standing on the edge of the writing world, or on the edge of success, don't allow fear to take over. Make up your mind to ignore the whole regiment—fear of the blank page, the computer, the editor, the critic ... fear that people will tell the truth, fear that they won't... Inundated with these thoughts, anticipating embarrassment and rejection rather than praise is natural. But like the downer drug routine becomes an ironclad habit, fear gets an iron clamp on writers. There's always the fear that we're unknowing about things we should know, that our ideas won't work, or we won't have any more ... Fear is always lurking around a writer.

Why won't it go away?

Susan Jefferies, Ph.D. explains in her book, *Feel the Fear And Do It Anyway*. Because "fear is a given, by virtue of the fact that we are human."

So, being inherent in human nature is a good excuse; it's natural to make mountains out of molehills. But let your dreams balloon above them. Every other writer suffers from fear too, more or less than you do. Accept the fact, and concentrate on reaching your goal.

The truest of truisms, "Live and learn," tells us life is a learning laboratory, failure our teacher. Accept this wisdom of the ages and focus on stretching your limits. Then when a rejection temporarily revives the fear virus, you'll discover more strength to attack it--and each time gain more confidence against it.

Emerson said, "By doing the thing you fear, death of fear is certain."

And by consensus of today's experts, it almost works. Besides, writers have no choice. If we're going to progress we must push our fears to the back burner and get on with it.

Once it seemed I would never conquer the army of butterflies so formidable when I was about to mail a submission, that necessary "thick skin" developing very slowly--until the day I read these words by *Writer's Digest* columnist, Art Spikol.

"There's no way of calculating how many terrific writers just sat back and allowed inactivity (out of fear) to make them anonymous."

I didn't want to be anonymous. I had something to say to the world.

You have something to say to the world. Writing is your chosen stage of performance. It is through literature that you hope to shine your light. If something very powerful has been inhibiting you, try a quick look back to break the hold. Twenty-twenty hindsight will prove that fear is but negative anticipation, and not always rooted in reality. You might also recognize conclusively that failure taught your most valuable lessons, as it teaches everybody. Had you been thinking you suffer alone?

Writing in Psychology Today, Tom Peters, author of *In Search of Excellence* (which sold seven million copies worldwide), says people must realize that failure is inevitable; and that everybody fears failure; they forget it's an invaluable teacher."

"The essence of everything one accomplishes in life, from the trivial to the grand, is failure." So stop fearing it.

Drop that four-letter word from your vocabulary.

BIRTH OF CONFIDENCE

Warm as a woolen blanket,
or luminous inner light,
breaking day with certainty
out of doubting night,
it surges into power
in accordance with my plan,
a singing swinging potent
force called confidence.
I can!

HOW TO SURVIVE IN THE WRITING WORLD

"The writing life can be a nightmare."

Those are the words of a prize-winning author teaching at a western university, "trying to get back to a normal life." He said his personal life was in "absolute chaos." And he needed "*regular* money."

For this man the highs and lows of a literary life didn't balance out. The joy of creating, freedom from mundane schedules, and being your own boss wasn't worth being out of sync with society. So he voluntarily "gave it up." To him being published didn't equate to success.

To ninety nine percent of his peers, however, published and success are synonymous; if they don't publish after an allotted time they consider themselves a failure, and give up.

Writing is essentially an act of courage. Comes an avalanche of rejection, the fire of inspiration flickers; resolve weakens; ambition fades. With repeated rejection latent insecurities surface, and many a promising hopeful gives up, before he realizes that he's not the exception.

Too many hopefuls give up too soon.

While preparing for your graduation from novice to professional, the most important lesson I would like you to learn is that rejection is the norm. Expect it; endure it; consider it training time. Without a doubt, the best selling author, or professional you admire went through the same boot camp; they endured, learned to accept rejection, and rose above it.

You can too. When you discover the dual requisite, that fine writing and *self-esteem* make the winning team—and that both depend on you—you are on your way.

I made the great discovery while hosting "The Writing World" (TV talk show). It readily became apparent that I was interviewing *survivors*. That polyglot of personality writers (a well-known psychic lecturer and author of thirty books, the popular western author of the "Leatherhand" series, a prize winning poet after publishing four hundred poems, a sixty-year-old novelist in first bloom of success...) all had one thing in common. To coin a word, "sticktuitiveness."

In researching their writing lives, their personal lives, their books, their backgrounds, the common thread of persistence became evident. So I asked each of them how they developed the staying power to survive the long years of disappointment and rejection.

What they all said, in one way or another, was "you have to keep up your confidence; do ANYTHING it takes."

However, when soliciting detailed recommendations for our viewers they mostly came in the form of what not to do. As a writing teacher I always believed that positive instruction was most helpful; but I wholly agreed with their advice in the negative. It packed a wallop. Following, in bold print, is the essence of it, and my comments.

Don't consider this advice, or anyone's, as gospel. Just consider it. Don't blindly follow, blindly believe everything an editor, or agent, or even the fellow-writer who has it made tells you—even if she does the same type of writing, on the same subject.

Especially not then. Editors don't buy carbon copy.

You do have to please the agent before she will agree to market your work. It is necessary to slant to the magazine or editor's philosophy, so he will read the manuscript. But if someone asks you to reverse your stand, change your message, or the whole structure of your book, think hard before you acquiesce. You almost bled that idea down on paper, maybe re-wrote or revised it twenty times, until you felt it was best expressed. If one person doesn't like it, even an experienced editor, your writing might not be at fault. Don't convict yourself on one person's testimony.

Seriously consider the words of the more experienced; but keep in mind that they are opinions not facts--and that editors have different opinions. Editors also change their minds; they change jobs, and are overruled at times.

I sent my first book to seventeen publishers before receiving a favorable report: "Interesting, well documented, we would consider if..." Making all the changes that editor dictated took me a month; he then took nine to decide it wouldn't do after all. The final consensus? The book was "not commercially viable."

The next editor I sent it to said, "Interesting material, well-written, has potential..." But she thought I should "eliminate a lot of the documentation, lighten it up, add humor."

Six months later I received a call while on vacation. My book had been passed to another editor, and now they wanted it *"better documented.*" I rushed home, and working night and day updated and re-inserted all the documentation I had taken out! Still, they didn't accept the book.

The next editor wanted it shortened. The next wanted it "beefed up." I heard "don't be afraid to tell it like it is," to "too caustic." This went on until even the anecdotes were dated. After four years I finally relegated that manuscript to the bottom drawer of the file cabinet, and went on to something else.

Writer's Digest once published "174 gems of advice from best selling authors." They were laughingly contradictory. One even said, "All advice is silly." After seven years on the seesaw of silly advice, I learned to listen to my "inner voice," rather than the conflicting chorus of outside ones.

Don't hibernate. No one ever makes it alone. A certain amount of networking and associating with peers is necessary to progress in any field. Writing may be called a lonely occupation, and many writers are loners; yet this holds true. Every step up, promotion, recognition (acceptance) results from the decision or action of somebody else.

Socializing just to rub shoulders with someone more successful is a waste of time; but occasionally getting out to conferences, seminars, and classes is beneficial. You make new contacts, gain new perspectives, and always learn *something*. And friendships with other writers are invaluable.

I'd been writing for years, part time, while working full time and raising a family (hoarding every precious minute, 4:30 a.m. or midnight) before I attended my first writing seminar. What they'd tell me I could get from books, couldn't I? Why waste all that time traveling and socializing?

Why indeed. At that first conference, sponsored by the National Writer's Association in Denver, I met a man with whom I had so much in common it was hard to believe. We both worked for The Government, in the Department of Defense, in public relations positions, and were both writing books about our experiences. My book, and my career, definitely profited from our exchange of information. Also, during that seminar I met an editor who agreed to read the book when it was finished!

Keep at it. Keep a regular schedule; let no excuses keep you from your computer or word processor; but get out once in a while and listen to pooled ideas. You won't take home a jeweled formula that will zoom you to instant success but often a foggy area is cleared. Always your mind is stretched.

Pearl Buck, who won both a Pulitzer and The Nobel Prize for literature, believed that a mind shrivels "if it hears only the echoes of its own thoughts." All the successful authors I interviewed, in one way or another, said the same thing. Get out and meet others in the writing business; make writer friends; occasionally attend a seminar. Keeping one's nose to the grindstone is stagnating.

Don't brood over rejections. A rejection letter is simply a no-sale; it is not a writing report card. If an editor writes on a printed rejection form, whether it's constructive criticism or even derogatory, study every word, and those invisible words between the lines. You may discover something you didn't know about publishing; you could find a key to that editor's philosophy. But don't berate yourself if you can't agree. And don't waste time worrying about it.

Maybe you sent it to the wrong publication. Maybe the editor was in a bad mood that day. Maybe he just didn't like it. As Andrew Greeley often emphasized, "Those who don't like your work could very well be wrong."

When first breaking out from church affiliated nonfiction Greeley was rejected coldly by commercial editors (and severely criticized by his peers). But he believed he had a message for the secular audience, and felt confident that he could write fiction. He was right and they were wrong.

The best of editors do not have crystal balls. Nor does any one editor hold your future in his or her hand.

Keep that thought in mind next time you receive a printed rejection. Refuse to be intimidated by little yellow, green, or pink pieces of paper. Don't count them. Don't brood over them. Negative responses often result from whims, fads, idiosyncrasies and circumstance, as well as faults—the editor's as well as yours.

Don't assume that breaking into print is your greatest challenge. Acceptance *isn't* always easier thereafter. Editors care little about how many other articles or stories you've sold if they don't like the one you send them. Your first sale involves luck and circumstance. So do all the others.

After years of writing technical reports, training manuals, government regulations, operating procedures, pamphlets, speeches, and press releases, I wrote a book for The Government (as an "overtime" assignment on the job). Uncle Sam published it, and *The Protocol Officer Handbook* was duly distributed to military installations across the U. S. and in several foreign countries. But after retiring, trying to make a living as a freelance writer I found that book didn't count. "The Government is not a *commercial* publisher."

During my long climb up the ladder I also learned that a magazine publishing record is not necessarily of help in the book market, unless it's on the same or a closely related subject.

In the writing game of matching manuscript to publisher you win when the editor you send it to likes it—and likes it well enough to convince the ruling powers in his publishing house that the target audience will too.

A good editor puts the publication first. "Money talks" is not just a cute phrase. What sells is what keeps the publishing house in business—and how the editor keeps her job. So if it isn't good or it isn't right (by that house standard) even sending to someone you know in the business can backfire. Consider what an editor friend told me.

"I prefer to receive from strangers. I tend to put off reading submissions from friends. Because if it's poor material, if it doesn't fit, or it isn't viable by the house yardstick, I'm put in a compromising position—the fear of losing a friend."

Don't be afraid to be a genius. For you <u>are</u> a potential genius. Each of us can be, when our fire is lighted. But many good writers of little faith hamstring their own spark by aping others, and worrying about what's "in." It's sad to watch a promising talent become a prisoner of the prevailing "right," and slip into mediocrity. We have only to look back in biography to discover that the writers in every category who came to be considered great were those who refused to conform to current trends (James Joyce, Walt Whitman, Hemingway). Instead of following the traditional path they dared to strike out in fields without a footprint, creating new paths.

Study, learn your craft, practice, keep a regular schedule, allot ample time for marketing ... And if you're still not satisfied with your progress, inhibitions to the wind! Let your genius arise.

Maybe you can't throw off enough restraints to emerge a genius. Perhaps you don't want to. Geniuses are eccentric, absent minded, anti-social They don't take time for daily-living generalities, nor waste time on mundane duties. They won't allow convention, or worry to hamstring their talent. Thus, they are able to develop it to the point excellence.

A full healthy confidence is a slow growing plant, requiring much nurturing. More than thirty years ago, when I chose a writing career I imagined that all I had to do was perfect my craft, write long hours, and get serious about marketing. In other words *work*. I wrote an article on that theme, and when it sold the first time out, I naively believed I was on my way. Little did I imagine the years of rejection to follow, or how hard it would be to keep believing in myself.

"The chief want in life," said Emerson, "is somebody who will make us do what we can." We writers must make ourselves do what we can.

Writing may not be, as often quoted, "... the hardest job in the world, with the possible exception of wrestling alligators," but to survive until you succeed does take power—physical power, mental power, and most of all the staying power of unfailing confidence in ourselves.

GENIUS

The one called genius
is not of special choice,
a mind given more,
or a favored son;
all God's children
are gifted to win.

Each an equal
inheritor,
executing our
individuality,
we travel
the earthly road
toward ultimate
possibility …

And those among us
who listen to the guiding
voice, and fully develop
the gift bestowed,
are called genius.

ABOUT THE AUTHOR

Internationally published author/poet **Delma Luben** began her career as a public relations professional with the U. S. Dept. of Defense. After retiring (as Chief of Protocol) she produced and hosted "The Writing World" TV show, and "Poetry for the Public" on radio. Executive editor, contributing editor *Writer's World,* writing teacher, mentor, motivational speaker, listed in national and international Who's Who directories, she was an IBC nominee for *Woman of the Year (1997).*